© 2024 Thomas LANDER. All rights reserved.

No part of this book may be reproduced, stored in a retrieval system, or transmitted in any form or by any means, electronic, mechanical, photocopying, recording, or otherwise, without the prior written permission of the publisher, except in the case of brief quotations embodied in critical reviews and certain other noncommercial uses permitted by copyright law.
For permissions requests, write to the publisher at the address below:

Publisher's Address:
Blue wild horse LLC
5830E 2ND ST, STE 7000
CASPER, WY 82609

Title : FBI WHO I AM
ISBN: 979-8-9919558-1-2

First Edition:2024

Disclaimer:

This book is not endorsed, sponsored, or affiliated with the FBI or the United States government. All information and opinions expressed in this book are those of the author and do not represent the official views or opinions of the FBI or any government agency.

The information provided in this book is for educational and informational purposes only. The author and publisher make no representations or warranties with respect to the accuracy or completeness of the contents of this book and specifically disclaim any implied warranties of merchantability or fitness for a particular purpose. Neither the author nor the publisher shall be liable for any loss or damage arising from the use of this book.

Credits photos: @FBI

Cover design by
Editing by Blue wild horse
Credits photo cover: South agency

Acknowledgments

I would like to express my deep gratitude to those who have supported and guided me throughout the creation of this book. Your expertise, insights, and encouragement have been invaluable.

Special thanks to the FBI for their services.

To my editor at Blue Wild Horse, your meticulous attention to detail and steadfast support have been instrumental in bringing this book to life.

Lastly, I offer my heartfelt homage to the brave FBI agents who work tirelessly to protect and serve. Your dedication and sacrifice are truly commendable.

With sincere appreciation,
Thomas LANDER

TABLE OF CONTENT

Structure of FBI 6

PART I

Chapter 1: The Origins of the FBI..8
Chapter 2: The Hoover Era...11
Chapter 3: The FBI and the Cold War...14
Chapter 4: The FBI and Civil Rights...17
Chapter 5: Modernization and the War on Terror..................................21
Chapter 6: The FBI in Popular Culture...28
Chapter 7: High-Profile Cases and Major Investigations..........................32
Chapter 8: International Cooperation and Global.................................40
Chapter 9: The future of the FBI..43
Chapter 10: Case Study: FBI vs. Cybercrime......................................46
Chapter 11: The Human Side of the FBI...50
Chapter 12 The FBI Academy..54
Chapter 13: The FBI's Role in Counterterrorism..................................59
Chapter 14 Evolution of the FBI and Computer Science............................62
Chapter 15: FBI's Role in Combating Organized Crime.............................65
Chapter 16: Special Agent Witness Protection....................................68
Chapter 17: Special Agent: Top Secret Cases.....................................71
Chapter 18: Future project of the FBI...75
Chapter 19: Inside the Mind of an FBI Agent 78

TABLE OF CONTENT

PART II

Chapter 1: Interview Special agent FBI...82
Chapter 2: Introduction type of specialized units................................89
Chapter 3: Interview SWAT Team 94
Chapter 4: Undercover Operation in the FBI.....................................100
Chapter 5: NIBRS and Operational Technology Division (OTD).....105
Chapter 6: Weapons of Mass Destruction (WMDs) 108
Chapter 7: The Behavioral Analysis Unit of the FBI........................111
Chapter 8: The FBI Laboratory..114
Chapter 9: FBI Artifacts...117
Chapter 10: National Memorial and Museum....................................119

Links...122
References..123

Federal Bureau of Investigation (FBI)

Director:
Current Director: Christopher Wray (since 2017).
- Nominated by the President, confirmed by the Senate, serves a 10-year term.
- Overall leadership and strategic direction of the FBI.

Deputy Director:
- Assists the Director in managing the FBI's day-to-day operations and pecial projects.

Executive Assistant Directors (EADs):
- Lead major branches such as Criminal, Cyber, and Intelligence Divisions.

2. Divisions and Offices

Headquarters:

- Located in Washington, D.C.
- Houses central leadership and administration functions.

Operational Divisions:

- Criminal Investigative Division: Handles organized crime, white-collar crime, violent crime, and drug trafficking.
- Cyber Division: Focuses on cyber threats, cybercrime investigations, and digital forensic analysis.
- Counterterrorism Division: Prevents and responds to terrorist activities, both domestic and international.

- Cyber Division: Focuses on cyber threats, cybercrime investigations, and digital forensic analysis.

- Counterterrorism Division: Prevents and responds to terrorist activities, both domestic and international.

- Counterintelligence Division: Protects against espionage, sabotage, and foreign intelligence threats.

- Intelligence Division: Collects, analyzes, and disseminates intelligence to support FBI operations.

Specialized Units:

- Hostage Rescue Team (HRT): Elite tactical unit for counterterrorism and hostage rescue missions.

- Critical Incident Response Group (CIRG): Provides rapid response to crises and special events.

Field Offices:

- 56 Field Offices: Located across major cities in the U.S.

- Resident Agencies: Smaller offices within the jurisdiction of Field Offices for local operations.

- Legal Attachés (Legats): Offices in U.S. embassies abroad to coordinate with international law enforcement.

3. Training and Development

FBI Academy:

- Location: Quantico, Virginia.

- Programs: Training for new agents, ongoing education for current agents, specialized courses.

- Physical and Tactical Training: Includes firearms proficiency, defensive tactics, and physical fitness.

Specialized Training Programs:

- Cyber Operations Training: Forensic analysis, network intrusion investigations.
- Behavioral Analysis Training: Techniques for profiling and understanding criminal behavior.
- Leadership Development: Courses to prepare agents for higher responsibility roles.

Chapter 1: The origins of the FBI

Initial Challenges and Missions

In the early 20th century, the United States faced significant challenges from criminal activities that transcended state boundaries. This era underscored the need for a specialized federal investigative body. Consequently, in 1908, the Bureau of Investigation, the precursor to the Federal Bureau of Investigation (FBI), was established to address these burgeoning criminal issues.

The inception of this pivotal institution can be attributed to the visionary efforts of Attorney General Charles Joseph Bonaparte. Driven by a fervent ambition to create an investigative arm within the Department of Justice (DOJ), Bonaparte, with the approval of President Theodore Roosevelt, formalized the Bureau of Investigation on July 26, 1908. Initially staffed by former Secret Service agents, the Bureau was tasked with adjudicating federal crimes and gathering intelligence on matters of national importance.

Under the leadership of its first Chief, Stanley Finch, the Bureau focused on combating white slavery, now recognized as human trafficking. During this formative period, the Bureau established its first field offices in major urban centers to address the growing tide of criminal activity. However, the nascent Bureau faced numerous challenges, including unclear jurisdictional boundaries and overlapping state and federal laws. Despite these obstacles, the Bureau quickly proved its worth by conducting high-profile investigations, including cases involving fraudulent land transactions and the oppressive system of peonage.

One of the Bureau's early successes was its investigation into the American Sugar Refining Company, also known as the Sugar Trust. This landmark case highlighted the Bureau's ability to conduct thorough and impactful investigations into economic corruption. Additionally, the Bureau's enforcement of the Mann Act of 1910, aimed at combating human trafficking for prostitution, demonstrated its commitment to addressing serious social issues.

The establishment of the Bureau marked a transformative period in American law enforcement, introducing increased federal oversight and coordination in the fight against crime. The Bureau's early achievements laid the groundwork for its evolution into the FBI, significantly influencing the landscape of American jurisprudence.

As the Bureau evolved, it became clear that a centralized federal investigative body was crucial for maintaining law and order across the United States. The foundational work of the Bureau of Investigation set the stage for the modern FBI's sophisticated and multifaceted operations, representing a pinnacle in American law enforcement.

The FBI agent emerged as a symbol of federal authority and investigative expertise. FBI agents, tasked with upholding federal law and protecting national security, represent the highest standards of law enforcement professionalism, dedication, and skill. The selection process for FBI agents is rigorous, involving thorough background checks, comprehensive training, and strict physical and psychological evaluations, ensuring only the most qualified individuals join the ranks. FBI agents serve as guardians of national security, equipped with extensive investigative powers and advanced resources. They operate with unwavering resolve and meticulous precision, navigating complex criminal landscapes with a steadfast commitment to justice. The FBI, as an institution, stands as a bastion against criminal machinations, upholding the rule of law and championing justice both domestically and internationally. It comprises a vast network of field offices, specialized units, and task forces, working synergistically to address threats ranging from cybercrime and terrorism to organized crime.

At its core, the FBI embodies the values of fidelity, bravery, and integrity, principles that are deeply ingrained in its organizational culture and exemplified by its dedicated agents and personnel. With a storied legacy spanning over a century, the FBI remains committed to safeguarding the nation's security and preserving the ideals upon which the republic was founded.

Three professional staff employees in the coiurtyard of FBI Headquarters in Washington, D.C.

Chapter 2: The Hoover Era
Hoover's Impact on the FBI's Stucture and Operations

John Edgar Hoover's name is synonymous with the Federal Bureau of Investigation (FBI), his tenure as its director from 1924 to 1972 marked by profound transformations, monumental successes, and deep controversies. Appointed by Attorney General Harlan Fiske Stone, Hoover inherited a Bureau plagued by corruption and inefficiency, yet he was resolute in his mission to overhaul the organization and restore public trust.

Hoover, a former librarian and dedicated public servant, instituted rigorous reforms to professionalize the Bureau. He established a centralized fingerprint file, expanded forensic laboratories, and introduced stringent training protocols at the newly founded FBI Academy. His emphasis on efficiency, discipline, and scientific investigation revolutionized the Bureau, enhancing its capabilities in combating crime.

Under Hoover's stewardship, the FBI's role expanded significantly. He underscored the importance of intelligence gathering and meticulous record-keeping, laying the groundwork for the Bureau's extensive files and dossiers. This focus on data collection and surveillance became a defining characteristic of his tenure.

Hoover's era saw the FBI involved in numerous high-profile cases and campaigns. During the Prohibition era, the Bureau aggressively pursued notorious gangsters like John Dillinger, Baby Face Nelson, and Pretty Boy Floyd, captivating the public's imagination and cementing the FBI's reputation as a formidable law enforcement entity. Another significant campaign was the fight against communism during the Red Scare.

Hoover, a staunch anti-communist, allocated substantial resources to identifying and neutralizing perceived communist threats within the United States. This included high-profile cases such as the conviction of Julius and Ethel Rosenberg for espionage.

Hoover was masterful in using the media to shape public perception of the FBI. He cultivated relationships with journalists and filmmakers, ensuring the Bureau's successes were well-publicized. This media strategy fostered a heroic image of the FBI and its agents, portrayed in radio shows, films, and comic books of the time, largely due to Hoover's influence.

Despite these achievements, Hoover's tenure was fraught with controversy. His authoritarian leadership style and use of the FBI to gather information on political adversaries and civil rights leaders drew significant criticism. Programs like COINTELPRO, targeting groups and individuals deemed subversive, later revealed to involve illegal surveillance, infiltration, and discrediting tactics. Hoover's obsession with power and control led to the accumulation of personal files on politicians, allegedly used to secure his prolonged leadership of the FBI, raising serious ethical and legal questions about the abuse of power within the Bureau.

Hoover's nearly five-decade leadership of the FBI was transformative. The Bureau grew in size, capability, and influence. While his contributions to its professionalization and modernization were significant, his legacy remains contentious, prompting ongoing debates about the balance between national security and civil liberties.

12/20/1930 First photo taken of President Hoover in the White House

Chapter 3: The FBI and the Cold War
The FBI's Role in Counterintelligence

The Cold War, an epoch of geopolitical tension between the United States and the Soviet Union, exerted a profound and enduring influence on myriad facets of American society, not least of which was the operational landscape of the FBI. In the crucible of this epochal confrontation, the Bureau's mandate underwent a significant metamorphosis, pivoting decisively towards the realm of counterintelligence and internal security, with a steadfast commitment to safeguarding the nation from the specter of espionage and subversion.

Emerging in the wake of World War II, the Cold War crystallized amidst the widening ideological schism between the capitalist West and the communist East. As the ideological chasm deepened, so too did the perceived threat of communist infiltration and espionage, galvanizing the FBI into a state of heightened vigilance and urgency under the stewardship of J. Edgar Hoover, a figure already predisposed towards apprehension regarding communist activities.

Under the aegis of Hoover's formidable leadership, the FBI ascended to the vanguard of domestic counterintelligence operations, assuming primacy in the relentless pursuit of suspected Soviet spies, the investigation of communist-front organizations, and the surveillance of American citizens suspected of engaging in subversive endeavors. Veiled in a cloak of secrecy, the Bureau's counterintelligence machinations remained clandestine, with the full extent of its operations only unveiled in the annals of history.

Throughout the Cold War epoch, a series of seminal espionage cases underscored the pivotal role of the FBI in counterintelligence:

The Rosenberg Case: The ignominious saga of Julius and Ethel Rosenberg, convicted of espionage for purportedly disseminating atomic secrets to the Soviet Union, captured the public imagination, epitomizing the prevailing climate of trepidation and paranoia surrounding communist infiltration.

The Alger Hiss Case: Alger Hiss, a former luminary of the State Department, found himself ensnared in the coils of controversy, accused of espionage in service of Soviet interests. His subsequent conviction for perjury, predicated largely on the testimony of Whittaker Chambers, constituted a resounding triumph for the FBI and underscored the pervasive reach of Soviet espionage.

Operation SOLO: A clandestine gambit orchestrated by the FBI, Operation SOLO entailed the infiltration of the Communist Party USA by informant Morris Childs, furnishing invaluable intelligence regarding Soviet activities and stratagems, thereby shaping the contours of U.S. policy vis-à-vis the Cold War adversary.

To streamline and fortify its endeavors in counterintelligence, the FBI established the Internal Security Division, an apparatus dedicated to the surveillance and investigation of subversive activities, both foreign and domestic. This division operated in concert with other federal agencies, including the CIA and NSA, fostering a symbiotic exchange of intelligence and a coordinated response to the Soviet menace.

The purview of the FBI's internal security apparatus extended pervasively across the American landscape, encompassing realms as diverse as education, labor unions, and entertainment. Employing a panoply of measures, including background checks and loyalty assessments, the Bureau endeavored to safeguard against the pernicious incursion of communist sympathizers into positions of influence within the fabric of society.

However, the fervor of the Cold War era engendered a climate of suspicion and apprehension, precipitating a palpable erosion of civil liberties. The specter of the Red Scare, epitomized by the House Un-American Activities Committee (HUAC) hearings and Senator Joseph McCarthy's zealous anti-communist crusade, cast a pall of fear and repression across the nation, impelling the FBI to wield its investigative prowess with an ever-heightened sense of urgency.

Amidst the crucible of the Cold War, the FBI emerged as an indomitable bulwark against the encroachments of espionage and subversion, crystallizing its identity as a preeminent counterintelligence agency. Yet, the crucible of this epochal confrontation also engendered a profound dialectic between security imperatives and civil liberties, a conundrum that continues to animate discourse surrounding the FBI's role in safeguarding the nation's security. As the curtains descended on the Cold War theater, the lessons gleaned from this epochal saga would continue to resonate within the corridors of the FBI, indelibly shaping its operational ethos and policy paradigms for generations to come. come.

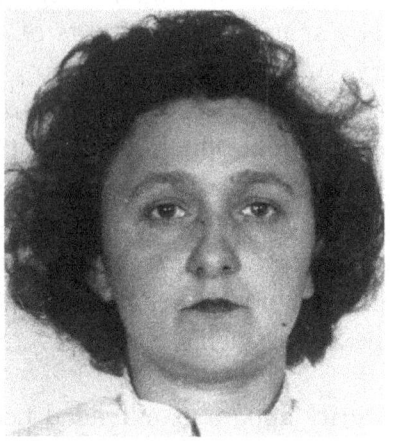
Ethel Rosenberg

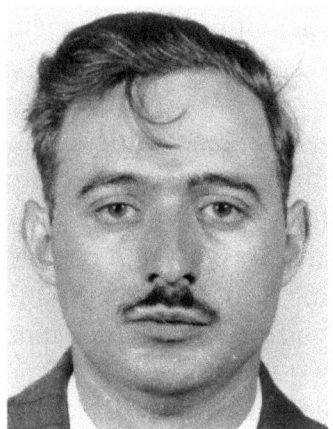
Julius Rosenberg

Chapter 4: The FBI and Civil Rights
The FBI's Role in Civil Rights Investigations

The Civil Rights Movement of the 1950s and 1960s was a transformative period in American history, marked by significant efforts to end racial segregation and discrimination. This era saw African Americans and other marginalized groups striving to achieve equal rights through nonviolent protest and legal challenges. The movement brought national attention to issues of racial injustice through key events such as the Montgomery Bus Boycott, the March on Washington, and the Selma to Montgomery marches.

The Role of the FBI in the Civil Rights Movement

During this time, the FBI played a complex and often controversial role. On one hand, the Bureau was tasked with investigating violations of civil rights laws, particularly in the South where racial violence and discrimination were most rampant. However, the FBI's involvement was not without significant controversy, as it also conducted extensive surveillance and covert operations against civil rights leaders and organizations.

Investigations into Civil Rights Violations

Under pressure from civil rights activists and the federal government, the FBI began to investigate numerous violations of civil rights laws. Some of the most notable cases included:

-The Murders of Civil Rights Workers in Mississippi (1964): During Freedom Summer, three civil rights workers—James Chaney, Andrew Goodman, and Michael Schwerner—were abducted and murdered by members of the Ku Klux Klan. The FBI's investigation, known as Mississippi Burning, eventually led to the conviction of several perpetrators, although many criticized the Bureau's initial response and the limited scope of justice achieved.

- The Bombing of the 16th Street Baptist Church in Birmingham, Alabama (1963)**: This horrific act of violence resulted in the deaths of four young African American girls. The FBI identified the perpetrators, who were members of a Klan splinter group, but initial prosecutions were delayed for years, highlighting the challenges and limitations of the Bureau's commitment to civil rights.

Suspicion and Criticism

Despite these investigations, many African Americans and civil rights activists viewed the FBI with suspicion. They believed that the Bureau was more focused on suppressing the civil rights movement than on protecting their rights. This skepticism was fueled by the FBI's Counter Intelligence Program, known as COINTELPRO.

COINTELPRO: A Controversial Program

COINTELPRO was initially launched in 1956 to disrupt communist activities in the United States. However, as the civil rights movement gained momentum, COINTELPRO expanded to target civil rights organizations, Black nationalist groups, and other perceived threats to national security. The program's tactics included surveillance, infiltration, and the dissemination of disinformation to discredit and disrupt these groups.

Targeting Civil Rights Leaders

Prominent figures and organizations targeted by COINTELPRO included Martin Luther King Jr., Malcolm X, the Southern Christian Leadership Conference (SCLC), and the Black Panther Party. The FBI's surveillance of civil rights leaders was extensive and invasive. Martin Luther King Jr., in particular, was subjected to intense scrutiny. FBI Director J. Edgar Hoover considered King a potential threat and directed the Bureau to monitor his activities closely. The FBI tapped King's phones, bugged his hotel rooms, and attempted to undermine his credibility by exposing alleged personal indiscretions.

These actions were intended to weaken the civil rights movement and prevent its leaders from gaining further influence. However, they also p drew significant criticism and raised serious ethical and legal concerns. The FBI's conduct during the civil rights era has been widely criticized. Many argue that the Bureau's actions were motivated by racial prejudice and political conservatism, rather than genuine concerns about national security.

Ethical and Legal Concerns

The use of COINTELPRO to disrupt lawful political activities and infringe upon the rights of American citizens is seen as a dark chapter in the Bureau's history. The exposure of COINTELPRO in the 1970s led to congressional investigations and increased oversight of the FBI. The Church Committee, a Senate committee that investigated abuses by intelligence agencies, condemned the FBI's actions and recommended reforms to prevent similar abuses in the future.

The Church Committee and Reforms

The Church Committee, officially known as the United States Senate Select Committee to Study Governmental Operations with Respect to Intelligence Activities, was established in 1975 to investigate abuses by the FBI, CIA, and other intelligence agencies. The committee's findings were damning, revealing widespread misconduct and abuse of power. The committee's final report condemned the FBI's actions during the civil rights era and recommended significant reforms to increase oversight and accountability.

Legacy and Impact

The legacy of the FBI's involvement in the civil rights era is complex. While the Bureau played a role in investigating civil rights violations, its actions against civil rights leaders and organizations damaged its reputation and highlighted the dangers of unchecked governmental power. The lessons learned from this period have influenced subsequent FBI policies and practices. Increased oversight, greater transparency, and a renewed commitment to protecting civil liberties are essential to ensuring that the Bureau operates within the bounds of the law and respects the rights of all citizens.

Modern Implications

The FBI's role in the civil rights movement and the controversies surrounding COINTELPRO illustrate the delicate balance between maintaining national security and protecting civil liberties. This chapter in the FBI's history serves as a reminder of the importance of accountability and the need for vigilance in safeguarding the rights of all Americans. In the years since the civil rights era, the FBI has implemented numerous reforms aimed at preventing similar abuses of power. These include the establishment of internal oversight mechanisms, increased transparency in operations, and a stronger emphasis on protecting civil liberties.

Continuing Challenges

Despite these reforms, the FBI continues to face challenges in balancing its dual roles of law enforcement and national security. Issues such as domestic terrorism, cyber threats, and international espionage require the Bureau to remain vigilant and proactive. However, the lessons of the

Chapter 5: Modernization and the War on Terror
Technological Advancements and Modernization

As the dawn of the new millennium heralded a paradigm shift in global dynamics, the FBI found itself confronting an ever-evolving tableau of threats and challenges. However, it was the seismic shockwaves of the 9/11 terrorist onslaught that catapulted the Bureau into an era of profound metamorphosis, precipitating sweeping transformations in its modus operandi, strategic imperatives, and overarching priorities.

Antecedent to the cataclysmic events of September 11, 2001, the FBI had embarked upon a trajectory of robust modernization initiatives. Driven by the imperatives of technological advancement, the burgeoning specter of cybercrime, and the inexorable globalization of criminal syndicates, the Bureau undertook concerted efforts to recalibrate its investigative arsenal and methodologies. Embracing the vanguard of technological innovation, the establishment of the FBI Laboratory Division emerged as a pivotal locus of this modernization drive, dedicated to the frontiers of forensic science and sophisticated investigative techniques.

At the forefront of this technological renaissance stood a constellation of pioneering advancements, including the expansion of the Combined DNA Index System (CODIS), the advent of the Integrated Automated Fingerprint Identification System (IAFIS), and the inception of the National Data Exchange (N-DEx) system. These groundbreaking tools endowed the FBI with unparalleled capacity to parse and analyze voluminous troves of data with alacrity and precision, thereby catalyzing breakthroughs in criminal identification and apprehension.

A poignant exemplar of the symbiotic nexus between technological innovation and investigative efficacy is encapsulated in the saga of the «Unabomber,» Ted Kaczynski. Leveraging the potency of computer databases, the FBI executed a tour de force of linguistic analysis, cross-referencing patterns in Kaczynski's manifesto with antecedent writings to effectuate his eventual apprehension. This seminal triumph underscored the burgeoning indispensability of data analytics and technological acumen in unraveling the tapestry of complex criminal conspiracies.

However, the crucible of September 11, 2001, served as an indelible crucible of transformation for the FBI, heralding a tectonic realignment of its operational ethos and strategic focus. The cataclysmic scale and audacious coordination of the terrorist assaults laid bare egregious lacunae in the nation's intelligence architecture and counterterrorism apparatus, galvanizing the Bureau into a frenetic frenzy of reevaluation and recalibration.

In the crucible of crisis, Director Robert Mueller assumed the mantle of leadership mere days preceding the epochal cataclysm, steering the Bureau through the crucible of existential peril with steely resolve and visionary sagacity. In the crucible of exigency, the FBI embarked upon a wholesale restructuring of its operational architecture, marshaling its finite resources towards the imperatives of preemptive counterterrorism and threat mitigation.

The heroic saga of Special Agent Lenny Hatton, a paragon of valor and selflessness, serves as a poignant testament to the unassailable fortitude and unwavering commitment of FBI agents in the face of unprecedented peril. His gallant sacrifice amidst the cauldron of chaos exemplifies the ethos of duty, honor, and sacrifice that pervades the hallowed halls of the Bureau.

In the crucible of post-9/11 recalibration, the FBI erected the edifice of the Counterterrorism Division, a bastion dedicated to the relentless pursuit and neutralization of terrorist threats, both domestic and international in scope. Augmented by the proliferation of Joint Terrorism Task Forces (JTTFs) across the nation, the Bureau forged synergistic partnerships with federal, state, and local agencies, fostering a seamless nexus of intelligence-sharing and collaborative response.

Yet, amidst the crucible of enhanced counterterrorism imperatives, the Bureau grappled with the concomitant imperatives of civil liberties and constitutional safeguards. The instantiation of so-called «assessments,» granting FBI agents carte blanche authority to deploy intrusive investi gatory techniques absent tangible predicates of criminality or national security threat, engendered fervent debate and scrutiny over the delicate equilibrium between security imperatives and individual liberties.

As the crucible of time marches inexorably forward, the FBI remains ensconced at the vanguard of national security and law enforcement, its trajectory irrevocably shaped by the crucible of 9/11 and the imperatives of an ever-evolving threat landscape.

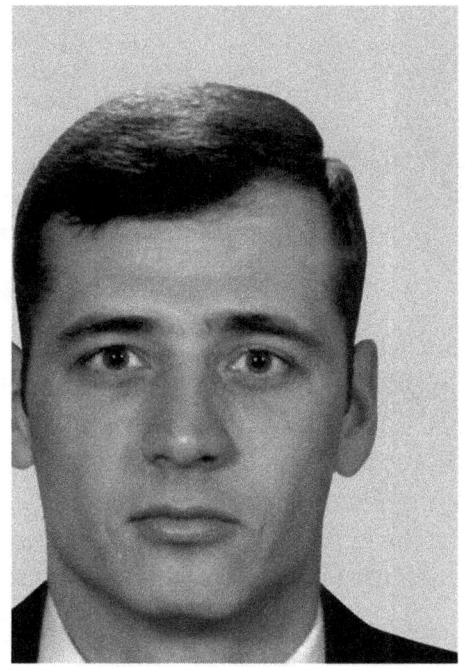

Leonard W.Hatton 1956 – 2001
(FBI source History Hall of Honor)

Several high-profile operations and investigations in the post-9/11 era highlighted the FBI's enhanced focus on counterterrorism:

The Capture of Khalid Sheikh Mohammed: In 2003, Pakistani authorities, in coordination with the CIA and FBI, captured Khalid Sheikh Mohammed, the mastermind behind the 9/11 attacks. His apprehension was a significant victory in the War on Terror. An FBI agent who participated in the interrogation process later recounted how Mohammed's capture provided critical intelligence that helped prevent further attacks.

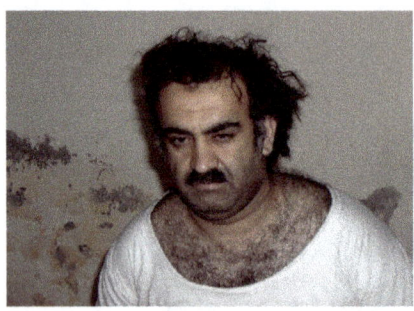

Khalid Sheikh Mohammed (sometimes also spelled Shaykh; also known by at least 50 pseudonyms; born 14 April 1965), often known by his initials KSM, is a Kuwaiti terrorist and the former Head of Propaganda for al-Qaeda. He is currently held by the United States at the Guantanamo Bay detention camp under terrorism-related charges. He was named as «the principal architect of the 9/11 attacks» in the 2004.

Operation Neptune Spear: The 2011 May 2 operation that led to the killing of Osama bin Laden involved extensive collaboration between the FBI, CIA, and U.S. military. The intelligence gathered from bin Laden's compound provided valuable insights into Al-Qaeda's operations. An FBI agent involved in analyzing the materials seized from the compound described the experience as «sifting through a treasure trove of intelligence,» which revealed new details about terrorist networks.

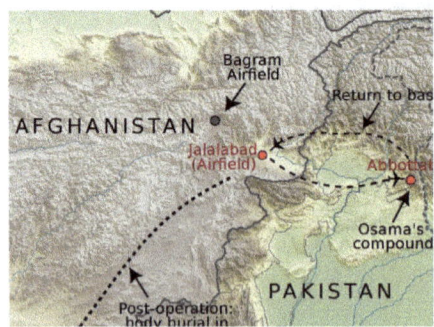 

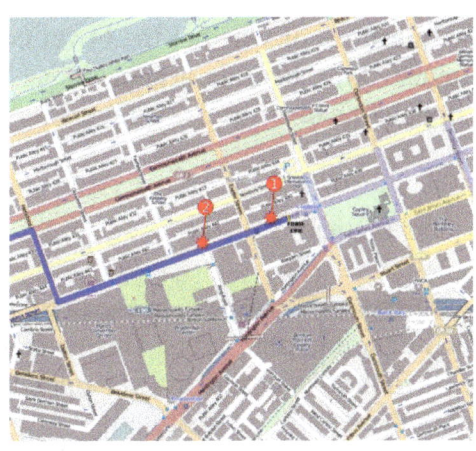

On April 18, 2013, the Federal Bureau of Investigation (FBI) released images of two suspects in the bombing. The two suspects were later identified as the Tsarnaev brothers. Later on the evening of April 18, the Tsarnaev brothers killed an MIT policeman (Sean Collier) and proceeded to commit a carjacking. They engaged in a shootout with police in nearby Watertown during which two officers were severely injured (one of the injured officers, Dennis Simmonds, died a year later). Tamerlan was shot several times, and his brother Dzhokhar ran him over while escaping in the stolen car. Tamerlan died soon thereafter.

An unprecedented manhunt for Dzhokhar Tsarnaev ensued, with thousands of law enforcement officers searching a 20-block area of Watertown. Residents of Watertown and surrounding communities were asked to stay indoors, and the transportation system and most businesses and public places closed. After a Watertown resident discovered Dzhokhar hiding in a boat in his backyard, Tsarnaev was shot and wounded by police before being taken into custody on the evening of April 19. During questioning, Dzhokhar said that he and his brother were motivated by the wars in Iraq and Afghanistan, that they were self-radicalized and unconnected to any outside terrorist groups, and that he was following his brother's lead. He said they learned to build explosive devices from the online magazine of al-Qaeda in the Arabian Peninsula. He also said they had intended to travel to New York City to bomb Times Square. He was convicted of 30 charges, including use of a weapon of mass destruction and malicious destruction of property resulting in death.

Two months later, he was sentenced to death, but the sentence was vacated by the United States Court of Appeals for the First Circuit. A writ of certiorari was granted by the Supreme Court of the United States, which considered the questions of whether the lower court erred in vacating the death sentence. After hearing arguments as United States v. Tsarnaev, the Court upheld the death penalty, reversing the First Circuit Court's decision.

Changes in Strategy and Tactics

The post-9/11 era saw the FBI adopt a more proactive and intelligence-driven approach to counterterrorism. This shift included the use of data analytics, surveillance, and undercover operations to identify and disrupt plots before they could be executed.
The FBI also placed greater emphasis on community outreach and engagement, working to build trust and cooperation with diverse communities across the United States. These efforts aimed to enhance the flow of information and improve the Bureau's ability to detect and prevent potential threats.

An example of the FBI's proactive approach is the case of Najibullah Zazi, an Afghan-American who planned to bomb the New York City subway system in 2009 September 10th. Zazi and others intended to obtain and assemble the remaining components of the bombs over the weekend and conduct the attack on Manhattan subway lines on Sept. 14, Sept. 15, or Sept. 16, 2009. Through intensive surveillance and intelligence work, the FBI was able to thwart the plot before it could be carried out. An agent involved in the operation recounted the meticulous and coordinated effort required to track Zazi's movements and gather the evidence needed to prevent the attack.

(credit photo Chris Schneider/The

The modernization of the FBI and its response to the 9/11 attacks marked a significant evolution in the Bureau's history. By embracing new technologies, restructuring its operations, and adopting a more proactive approach, the FBI positioned itself to better address the complex and evolving threats of the 21st century. The lessons learned from this period continue to shape the Bureau's strategies and priorities, ensuring that it remains a vital force in protecting national security.

Chapter 6: The FBI in Popular Culture
Public Perception and Media Influence

From its inception, the FBI has captured the public's imagination, becoming a staple in American popular culture. Through literature, film, and television, the Bureau has been depicted in various lights, shaping public perception and influencing how the FBI is viewed by society.

Introduction to the FBI's Cultural Impact

The FBI's image in popular culture is a blend of fact and fiction. Early depictions often emphasized the heroic and incorruptible nature of FBI agents, presenting them as guardians of law and order. Over time, these portrayals have evolved, reflecting changes in society's views on law enforcement and the complexities of the Bureau's work.

Depictions in Literature and Film

Literature and film have played significant roles in shaping the FBI's image. Early 20th-century novels and films often depicted G-Men (short for «Government Men») as fearless crime-fighters. Movies like «G-Men» (1935), starring James Cagney, glorified the FBI's battle against gangsters during the Prohibition era.
One of the most famous literary works featuring the FBI is Thomas Harris's «The Silence of the Lambs» (1988). The novel, and its film adaptation, introduced the world to Special Agent Clarice Starling and her pursuit of the serial killer Buffalo Bill, with the help of the imprisoned Dr. Hannibal Lecter. The character of Starling, portrayed by Jodie Foster in the 1991 film, became an iconic representation of the FBI agent as intelligent, determined, and morally complex.

Television Shows and the FBI

Television has further cemented the FBI's presence in popular culture.

Shows like «The X-Files» (1993-2002) combined elements of science fiction with procedural drama, following FBI agents Fox Mulder and Dana Scully as they investigated paranormal phenomena. The show's blend of mystery, conspiracy theories, and government intrigue resonated with audiences, making it a cultural phenomenon.

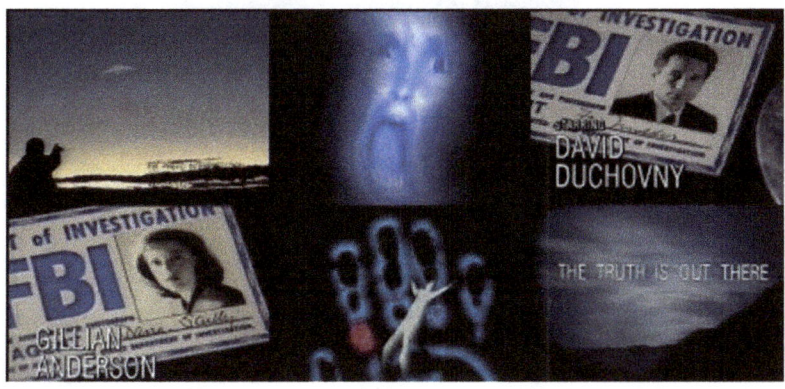

Another notable series is «Criminal Minds» (2005-2020), which focuses on the FBI's Behavioral Analysis Unit (BAU). The show delves into the psychological profiling of serial killers and other criminals, providing a dramatized look at the investigative techniques used by the Bureau.

Public Perception and Media Influence

The portrayal of the FBI in popular culture has significantly influenced public perception. Positive depictions have often bolstered the Bureau's reputation, portraying agents as heroes who protect society from dangerous criminals. However, negative portrayals, especially those highlighting issues of corruption or overreach, have also shaped critical views of the FBI.

One example of this duality can be seen in the contrasting films «Mississippi Burning» (1988) and «The Black Klansman» (2018). «Mississippi Burning,» based on true events, depicts FBI agents investigating the murder of civil rights workers in the 1960s, showcasing the Bureau's role in combating racial violence. In contrast, «The Black Klansman,» which tells the story of an African-American detective infiltrating the Ku Klux Klan with the help of a Jewish colleague, offers a more critical view of law enforcement and its historical challenges with race.

Real-life Agents and Their Stories

The stories of real-life FBI agents have also captivated the public. Figures like Melvin Purvis, who famously led the manhunt for notorious criminals like John Dillinger and Pretty Boy Floyd in the 1930s, became legends in their own right. Purvis's exploits were widely covered in the media, contributing to the mythos of the FBI agent as a relentless pursuer of justice.

The FBI's Media Relations and Public Engagement

Recognizing the power of media in shaping public perception, the FBI has actively engaged with filmmakers, authors, and journalists. The Bureau has often provided technical advice and access to enhance the accuracy of its portrayals. This collaboration helps ensure that the depiction of FBI operations in media is grounded in reality, even if dramatized for entertainment purposes.

Additionally, the FBI has used media to its advantage by producing its own content. The Bureau's public website and various social media platforms provide updates on ongoing cases, historical information, and educational resources, allowing the FBI to control its narrative and engage directly with the public.

he FBI's presence in popular culture has evolved over the decades, reflecting changes in societal attitudes and the Bureau's own development. From the heroic G-Men of the early 20th century to the complex, nuanced characters of modern media, the portrayal of the FBI continues to captivate and influence public perception. As the Bureau navigates the challenges of the 21st century, its image in popular culture will undoubtedly continue to evolve, shaping how future generations view one of America's most storied institutions.

Chapter 7: High-Profile Cases and Major Investigations

High-Profile Cases

Throughout its history, the FBI has been at the forefront of investigating some of the most high-profile cases in American history. These cases have often captivated the public's attention, showcasing the Bureau's investigative prowess and, at times, highlighting its challenges and controversies.

High-profile cases typically involve significant public interest, extensive media coverage, and substantial resource allocation from the FBI. These cases not only test the Bureau's investigative capabilities but also its ability to manage public perception and navigate complex legal and ethical issues.

The FBI's role in such cases underscores its importance in maintaining national security and public safety. From the Lindbergh kidnapping in the 1930s to more recent incidents of terrorism and cybercrime, the Bureau has demonstrated its expertise in solving intricate and often dangerous cases. The scrutiny that comes with high-profile investigations also requires the FBI to uphold the highest standards of professionalism and integrity.

Despite the challenges, the FBI's handling of these cases has often led to significant advancements in investigative techniques and federal law enforcement practices. Each case, with its unique set of circumstances and obstacles, contributes to the evolving narrative of the FBI's mission to protect and serve the United States.

The Lindbergh Kidnapping

One of the earliest high-profile cases that cemented the FBI's reputation as a premier investigative agency was the kidnapping of Charles Lindbergh Jr., the 20-month-old son of famed aviator Charles Lindbergh, in 1932. This tragic event not only captivated the nation but also brought significant changes to federal law enforcement in the United States.

On the evening of March 1, 1932, Charles Lindbergh Jr. was abducted from his crib in the Lindbergh family home near Hopewell, New Jersey. The kidnappers left a ransom note demanding $50,000, which was an astronomical sum during the Great Depression. The disappearance of the «Eaglet,» as he was affectionately known, shocked the American public, sparking an intense media frenzy and widespread search efforts.

The initial investigation was conducted by local and state authorities, but as the case grew more complex and crossed state lines, it became evident that federal intervention was necessary. The case was taken over by the Federal Bureau of Investigation (then known as the Bureau of Investigation), under the leadership of Director J. Edgar Hoover. The FBI's involvement marked a significant turning point in the investigation, bringing more resources and advanced techniques to bear on solving the crime.

The FBI coordinated with various law enforcement agencies, including the New Jersey State Police and the New York Police Department. They followed numerous leads, analyzed ransom notes, and interviewed countless witnesses. Despite these efforts, the case remained unresolved for several months. The Lindberghs paid the ransom, but their son was not returned. Tragically, on May 12, 1932, the body of Charles Lindbergh Jr. was discovered in a wooded area near the family home, ending any hope of his safe return.

The investigation continued, focusing on finding those responsible for the heinous crime. A major breakthrough came in 1934 when a marked ransom bill was traced to Bruno Richard Hauptmann, a German immigrant living in the Bronx, New York. Hauptmann was arrested and found to have a significant amount of the ransom money in his possession. Further evidence, including handwriting analysis and the discovery of materials linking him to the construction of the homemade ladder used in the kidnapping, led to his conviction. Hauptmann was found guilty of first-degree murder and was executed in 1936.

The Lindbergh kidnapping had far-reaching implications beyond the tragic loss of a young life. The case highlighted the limitations of local and state law enforcement in handling crimes of such magnitude and complexity. In response, Congress passed the «Lindbergh Law» in

1932, which made kidnapping across state lines a federal offense. This legislation significantly expanded the FBI's jurisdiction and set a precedent for federal involvement in major criminal cases.

The successful investigation and prosecution of the Lindbergh kidnapping boosted public confidence in the FBI and established its reputation as a formidable force in law enforcement. The case also underscored the importance of forensic science, interagency cooperation, and meticulous investigative work in solving complex crimes.

In conclusion, the kidnapping of Charles Lindbergh Jr. was a landmark case in American criminal history. It brought about crucial changes in federal law enforcement, underscored the need for a coordinated approach to solving major crimes, and solidified the FBI's role as a key player in the fight against crime. The legacy of the Lindbergh case continues to influence modern investigative techniques and policies, reflecting its enduring impact on the justice system in the United States.

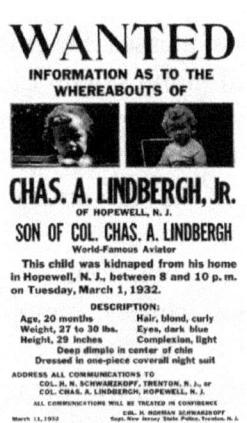

Charles Lindgergh

The Capture of John Dillinger

John Dillinger, one of America's most notorious criminals during the Great Depression, was a key target for the FBI in the 1930s. Dillinger's string of bank robberies and daring escapes from jail made him a legendary figure, but also a significant threat to public safety.

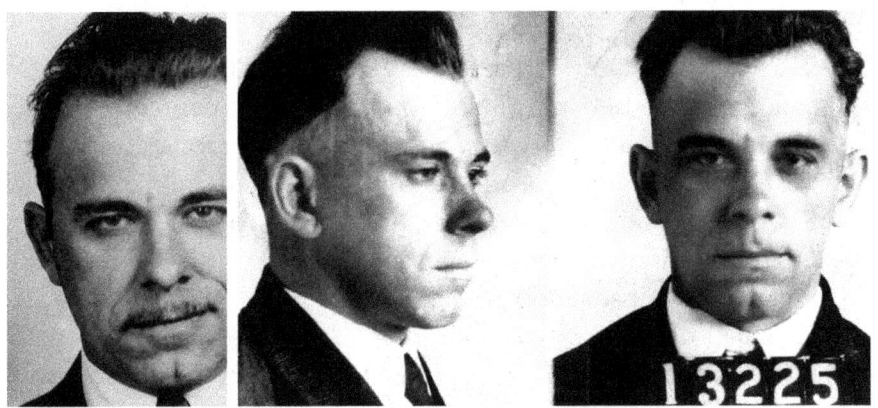

John Herbert Dillinger

The FBI's relentless pursuit of Dillinger culminated in his capture and eventual death in 1934. An anecdote from this case involves Special Agent Melvin Purvis, who led the operation that cornered Dillinger outside the Biograph Theater in Chicago. Purvis's calm demeanor and strategic planning were pivotal in the successful apprehension of Dillinger, demonstrating the effectiveness of well-coordinated law enforcement efforts.

The Watergate Scandal

The Watergate scandal of the 1970s marked a significant turning point in American politics and law enforcement. It all began with a seemingly minor incident: a break-in at the Democratic National Committee headquarters located in the Watergate Complex in Washington, D.C., on June 17, 1972. However, what initially appeared to be a straightforward burglary soon unraveled into a complex web of political espionage, sabotage, and a high-level cover-up that shook the very foundations of the United States government.

The scandal gained momentum when it was discovered that the break-in was not an isolated incident but part of a broader campaign of political spying and dirty tricks orchestrated by members of President Richard Nixon's re-election committee. As journalists Bob Woodward and Carl Bernstein of The Washington Post delved deeper into the story, aided by their secret informant known as «Deep Throat,» they uncovered connections leading back to the highest echelons of power in the Nixon administration.

The FBI's role in investigating Watergate was critical and showcased the bureau's capability and integrity in handling politically sensitive cases. FBI agents conducted numerous interviews, meticulously analyzed a vast array of evidence, and followed a complex money trail. This financial investigation revealed that funds used for the break-in were linked to the Committee to Re-elect the President (CREEP), further implicating Nixon's close aides and advisors.

As the investigation progressed, it became evident that there was an orchestrated effort to obstruct justice and conceal the involvement of White House officials. The turning point came when it was revealed that Nixon had installed a secret taping system in the Oval Office, which recorded all conversations. Subpoenas for these tapes led to a protracted legal battle, culminating in the Supreme Court's unanimous decision in United States v. Nixon, which ordered the President to release the tapes. The tapes provided undeniable evidence of Nixon's involvement in the cover-up and his attempts to use federal agencies, including the FBI, to thwart the investigation.

The Watergate scandal ultimately led to the resignation of President Richard Nixon on August 8, 1974, making him the first and only U.S. president to resign from office. The scandal had far-reaching consequences, leading to widespread public cynicism about politics and prompting reforms aimed at increasing transparency and accountability in government.

Throughout the Watergate scandal, the FBI's steadfast commitment to impartial investigation and adherence to the rule of law were crucial. The bureau's work highlighted the importance of maintaining its independence from political influence, ensuring that justice is served without regard to the stature or position of those involved. The Watergate investigation underscored the FBI's vital role in preserving the integrity of the democratic process and upholding the principles of justice and accountability.

A photo of the Watergate Complex

The FBI's role in investigating Watergate was critical. Agents conducted interviews, analyzed evidence, and followed the money trail that ultimately implicated top White House officials. The

The Unabomber Investigation

The Unabomber case, spanning nearly two decades, involved a series of bombings by Ted Kaczynski, a former mathematics professor with a deep-seated disdain for modern technology and industrial society. Kaczynski's bombs killed three people and injured 23 others, instilling fear across the nation.

Pieces of one of Ted Kaczynski's-bombs

The breakthrough in the investigation came when Kaczynski's manifesto was published in major newspapers. His brother, David Kaczynski, recognized the writing style and alerted the FBI. This led to Ted Kaczynski's arrest in 1996. The case highlighted the importance of public cooperation and the role of behavioral analysis in solving complex criminal cases.

The 1993 World Trade Center Bombing

The bombing of the World Trade Center in 1993 February 26 was a precursor to the larger attacks on September 11, 2001. The explosion in the underground parking garage killed six people and injured over a thousand, shaking the nation's sense of security.

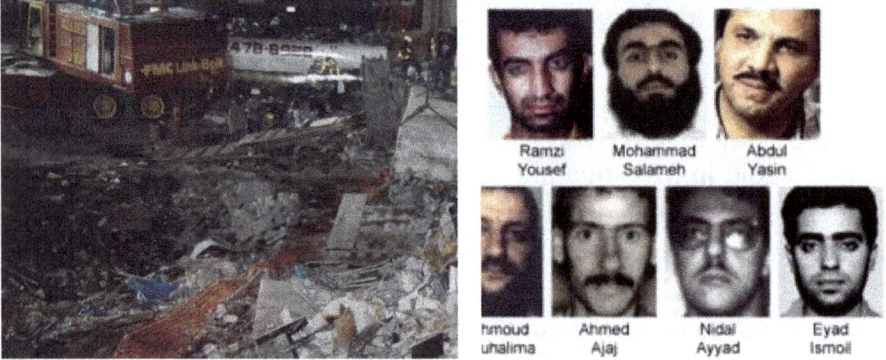

The conspirators in the bombing

The FBI's investigation led to the arrest and conviction of several conspirators, including Ramzi Yousef, the mastermind behind the attack. The case underscored the growing threat of international terrorism and the need for enhanced intelligence and counterterrorism measures.

The Boston Marathon Bombing

The Boston Marathon bombing in 2013 was a significant domestic terrorist attack that tested the FBI's capabilities in handling real-time threats. Two bombs exploded near the marathon's finish line, killing three people and injuring hundreds.

Spectators helping victims soon after the attack

The FBI played a central role in the investigation and subsequent manhunt for the perpetrators, Tamerlan and Dzhokhar Tsarnaev. Utilizing surveillance footage, forensic evidence, and public assistance, the Bureau swiftly identified the suspects. The dramatic apprehension of Dzhokhar Tsarnaev in a residential neighborhood highlighted the FBI's ability to coordinate complex operations under intense public scrutiny.
High-profile cases and major investigations have been pivotal in shaping the FBI's reputation and operational strategies. These cases exemplify the Bureau's resilience, adaptability, and unwavering commitment to justice. Whether tackling organized crime, terrorism, or sophisticated cyber threats, the FBI has continually evolved its methods and techniques to stay ahead of criminal activity.
As the FBI continues to confront new challenges in an ever-changing landscape, the lessons learned from these landmark investigations remain integral to its mission of safeguarding the American public. The Bureau's ability to adapt to new technologies, manage extensive media scrutiny, and navigate complex legal and ethical issues ensures that it remains a robust and effective force in law enforcement.
The enduring impact of these high-profile cases underscores the importance of continuous improvement and vigilance within the FBI, solidifying its role as a cornerstone of American national security and public safety.

Chapter 8: International Cooperation and Global Counterterrorism and Intelligence Sharing, Cybersecurity and Transnational Crime

In an increasingly interconnected world, the FBI has expanded its reach beyond U.S. borders to address transnational threats and collaborate with foreign partners. International cooperation plays a vital role in the Bureau's efforts to combat terrorism, cybercrime, organized crime, and other global challenges.

The FBI's mandate extends beyond national borders, necessitating close collaboration with law enforcement agencies, intelligence services, and other organizations worldwide. Through international cooperation, the FBI can gather intelligence, conduct investigations, and apprehend criminals operating across multiple jurisdictions.

Interpol, the International Criminal Police Organization, serves as a central hub for international law enforcement cooperation. The FBI works closely with Interpol and its member countries to share information, coordinate operations, and track fugitives and criminals across borders. Other international organizations, such as Europol and the United Nations Office on Drugs and Crime (UNODC), also play crucial roles in facilitating global partnerships. These collaborations enhance the Bureau's ability to address crimes that transcend national boundaries.
The FBI collaborates with foreign law enforcement agencies through joint task forces and bilateral agreements. These partnerships enable the Bureau to leverage the expertise and resources of international counterparts in specific regions or areas of expertise. Joint task forces tackle a wide range of issues, from counterterrorism and drug trafficking to human trafficking and cybercrime. Bilateral agreements facilitate more streamlined cooperation, allowing for more effective joint operations and information sharing.

In the wake of the 9/11 attacks, the FBI intensified its efforts to combat terrorism through international cooperation. The Bureau works closely with foreign intelligence agencies to gather and share intelligence on terrorist threats, disrupt plots, and apprehend suspects. Information sharing and joint operations have led to numerous successful counterterrorism efforts, preventing attacks and dismantling terrorist networks. This collaborative approach is essential for addressing the global nature of terrorism.

Cybercrime knows no borders, making international cooperation essential in combating online threats. The FBI collaborates with foreign partners to investigate cyberattacks, dismantle cybercriminal networks, and enhance cybersecurity measures. Joint efforts target a variety of cybercrimes, including hacking, data breaches, ransomware attacks, and online fraud. By working together, international partners can more effectively trace and disrupt cybercriminal activities.

Despite the benefits of international cooperation, challenges and limitations exist. Differences in legal systems, cultural norms, and language barriers can hinder effective collaboration. Concerns about sovereignty, privacy, and data protection also complicate information sharing and joint investigations. Moreover, geopolitical tensions and diplomatic considerations may strain international partnerships, affecting the flow of intelligence and cooperation. These obstacles require careful navigation to maintain effective international relations.

Despite these challenges, numerous success stories demonstrate the effectiveness of international cooperation. For example, the joint investigation into the 2017 WannaCry ransomware attack, which affected hundreds of thousands of computers worldwide, led to the identification and indictment of North Korean hackers. Similarly, the FBI's collaboration with European law enforcement agencies resulted in the takedown of the DarkMarket dark web marketplace in 2021, disrupting a major hub for illegal activities. These cases highlight the tangible benefits of global partnerships in addressing complex transnational crimes.

International cooperation and global partnerships are indispensable in the FBI's efforts to address transnational threats and protect national security. By working closely with foreign counterparts, the Bureau enhances its investigative capabilities, fosters information sharing, and promotes collective action against common threats. As challenges evolve and new threats emerge, the FBI remains committed to strengthening its international relationships and advancing global security. This ongoing commitment ensures that the FBI remains a robust and effective force in the fight against global crime.

Chapter 9: The Future of the FBI
Investing in Training and Professional Development

As the world evolves, so too must the FBI. The Bureau faces a rapidly changing landscape of threats and challenges, necessitating adaptation, innovation, and strategic planning. The future of the FBI lies in its ability to embrace technological advancements, adapt to emerging threats, promote diversity and inclusion, engage with the public, uphold ethical standards, and invest in its workforce.

The FBI operates in a dynamic environment shaped by advances in technology, globalization, shifting demographics, and evolving geopolitical dynamics. To remain effective in fulfilling its mission of protecting the American people and upholding the Constitution, the Bureau must anticipate and respond to these changes proactively.

The digital age presents both opportunities and challenges for law enforcement. Technological advancements have revolutionized crime-fighting techniques, but they have also expanded the scope and complexity of cyber threats. The FBI must continue to invest in cybersecurity capabilities, leverage advanced analytics and artificial intelligence, and collaborate with industry partners to stay ahead of cybercriminals.

As the nature of crime evolves, so too must the FBI's strategies and tactics. From terrorism and organized crime to cyber threats and emerging technologies like artificial intelligence and biotechnology, the Bureau must remain vigilant and adaptable. By prioritizing intelligence-led policing, building strategic partnerships, and fostering innovation, the FBI can effectively address emerging threats to national security and public safety.

A diverse and inclusive workforce is essential for the FBI to effectively serve the diverse communities it protects. By recruiting and retaining a diverse range of talent, promoting equity and inclusion, and fostering a culture of respect and belonging, the Bureau can better understand and address the needs and concerns of all Americans. Diversity of thought and experience strengthens the FBI's ability to tackle complex challenges and promote justice for all.

Building trust and collaboration with the public is essential for effective law enforcement. The FBI must prioritize community engagement, transparency, and accountability to foster positive relationships with the communities it serves. By partnering with local law enforcement agencies, community organizations, and civic leaders, the Bureau can enhance public safety and strengthen community resilience against crime and extremism.

Maintaining the highest ethical standards is paramount for the FBI to uphold the rule of law and earn public trust. The Bureau must adhere to its core values of fidelity, bravery, and integrity in all aspects of its operations. This includes ensuring accountability for misconduct, respecting civil liberties and human rights, and upholding the principles of justice and fairness in every interaction

A skilled and well-trained workforce is the backbone of the FBI's success. The Bureau must invest in continuous training, education, and professional development to equip its agents and analysts with the knowledge, skills, and tools needed to address evolving threats and challenges. By fostering a culture of lifelong learning and innovation, the FBI can adapt to changing circumstances and excel in its mission.

The future of the FBI is bright, but it requires bold leadership, strategic vision, and a commitment to excellence. By embracing technological innovation, adapting to emerging threats, promoting diversity and inclusion, engaging with the public, upholding ethical standards, and investing in its workforce, the Bureau can continue to fulfill its mission of protecting the American people and upholding the Constitution in the 21st century and beyond.

Chapter 10: Case Study: FBI vs. Cybercrime

FBI's Role in Combating Cybercrime

Cybercrime poses one of the most significant threats to national security and economic stability in the 21st century. As technology advances, so too do the methods and sophistication of cybercriminals. This case study examines the FBI's efforts to combat cybercrime, focusing on Operation Ghost Click, a landmark investigation into a global cybercriminal network.

Cybercrime encompasses a wide range of illicit activities conducted over the internet, including hacking, identity theft, fraud, ransomware attacks, and espionage. These crimes pose serious risks to individuals, businesses, and governments, with far-reaching consequences for privacy, financial security, and national security.

Cyber threats have evolved significantly in recent years, becoming more complex, diverse, and pervasive. Cybercriminals exploit vulnerabilities in software, networks, and systems to steal data, disrupt services, and extort money. The rise of cryptocurrency, anonymous networks, and sophisticated hacking tools has made it easier for cybercriminals to operate with impunity.

The FBI plays a central role in investigating and combating cybercrime, leveraging its technical expertise, investigative resources, and partnerships with domestic and international stakeholders. The Bureau's Cyber Division leads efforts to identify, disrupt, and dismantle cybercriminal networks, working closely with other federal agencies, law enforcement partners, private sector entities, and foreign counterparts. Combatting cybercrime presents unique challenges for law enforcement, including jurisdictional issues, attribution problems, and the rapidly evolving nature of digital threats. The FBI employs a multifaceted approach to address these challenges, focusing on proactive intelligence gathering, capacity building, public awareness campaigns, and targeted enforcement actions.

Operation Ghost Click was a joint FBI-led investigation into an international cybercriminal network responsible for infecting millions of computers worldwide with malware known as DNSChanger. The malware hijacked users' internet connections, redirected web traffic to fraudulent websites, and generated millions of dollars in illicit profits through click fraud schemes.

The operation, which began in 2011, involved coordinated efforts by the FBI, international law enforcement agencies, and private sector partners. Through meticulous forensic analysis, undercover operations, and legal cooperation, investigators identified and apprehended the leaders of the cybercriminal ring, dismantling their infrastructure and securing critical evidence for prosecution.

The success of Operation Ghost Click underscores the importance of international cooperation and the FBI's ability to adapt to the evolving landscape of cyber threats. By leveraging advanced technology and fostering global partnerships, the FBI continues to play a crucial role in protecting the digital infrastructure and ensuring the security of individuals, businesses, and governments worlwide.

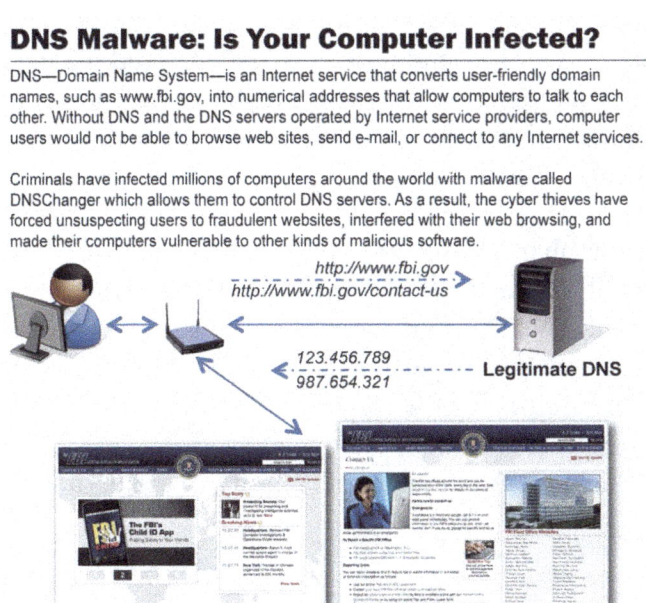

Press: FBI shuts down 'Ghost Click' botnet of 4m PCs as seven face charges

The US FBI and the Estonian police have disabled a botnet of more than 4m infected PCs as part of «Operation Ghost Click», in which six Estonians and one Russian have been charged with a number of cybercrime offences relating to fake adverts and misdirected web links.People trying to get to the US Internal Revenue Service and to Apple's iTunes store would instead be redirected to fake sites, and normal web pages would be served ads via the botnet instead of the proper advertisers.The scam, begun in 2007, earned about $14m (£8.7m) and infected computers in more than 100 countries with malware called «DNSChanger» which would alter the DNS settings on the machine so that requests to visit particular sites would instead be redirected to others serving ads from the criminals' partners. Both Windows PCs and Apple Macintosh machines could be affected.Six Estonians were arrested on Tuesday, Manhattan US attorney Preet Bharara said, while the seventh person, a Russian citizen, remains at large. Each of the accused faces five criminal charges including conspiracy to commit wire fraud and computer intrusion, which in the US carries a maximum 30-year prison sentence.

Operation Ghost Click served as a poignant illustration of the critical role that international collaboration, public-private partnerships, and pioneering investigative methodologies play in the ongoing battle against cybercrime. This landmark case underscored the imperative for bolstered information dissemination, heightened technical proficiency, and fortified legal frameworks to effectively counteract the ever-evolving landscape of global cyber threats.

The FBI's triumphant prosecution of Operation Ghost Click conveyed an unequivocal message to cyber malefactors: the long arm of justice extends universally. Through the strategic utilization of its abundant resources, unparalleled expertise, and steadfast alliances, the Bureau remains at the forefront of the crusade against cyber malfeasance, safeguarding the interests of individuals, enterprises, and vital infrastructure amidst the burgeoning interconnectivity of the digital age.

Chapter 11: The Human Side of the FBI
The FBI Family

Behind the sensational headlines and high-profile investigations, the FBI stands as a bastion of devoted individuals who confront challenges, make profound sacrifices, and exhibit unwavering courage in the line of duty. This chapter delves into the intricacies of the human dimension within the FBI, shedding light on narratives of valor, selflessness, fortitude, and the profound impact of FBI agents and personnel on the fabric of their communities.

At its essence, the FBI is a mosaic of individuals—agents, analysts, support staff, and their families—united by a shared commitment to safeguarding and serving their nation. Peering into the human core of the FBI unveils the personal journeys, sentiments, and impetuses that propel its members towards excellence in their respective roles.

Across its storied history, the FBI has borne witness to acts of extraordinary valor and self-sacrifice enacted by its agents and personnel. From confronting armed felons to infiltrating clandestine terrorist networks, these individuals willingly put their lives on the line to uphold the sanctity of law and protect the welfare of the public. Tales such as that of Special Agent Edwin R. Woodriffe Jr., tragically slain while apprehending a bank robber in 2007, serve as poignant reminders of the perils and sacrifices endured by those adorned with the bureau's badge. These accounts underscore the depths of dedication and the extent to which individuals are willing to go to preserve justice and order.
Beneath the veneer of every FBI agent lies a steadfast network of support—comprising family members, friends, and colleagues—whose unwavering encouragement, understanding, and resilience provide sustenance amidst the rigors of duty. The unspoken sacrifices borne by the families of FBI personnel, from missed celebrations to nocturnal

vigils by the telephone, resonate deeply. Their steadfast fortitude undergirds agents and personnel, enabling them to discharge their responsibilities with steadfast dedication and resolve. Moreover, this familial support system serves as a cornerstone in maintaining the mental and emotional well-being of those who serve, providing a sanctuary amid the challenges and stresses inherent in their roles.

The life of an FBI agent is a tapestry woven with challenges and triumphs, marked by extended hours, high-stakes investigations, and perpetual pressure to excel. Agents navigate the labyrinthine complexities of undercover operations, surveillance, and courtroom testimony, all while endeavoring to strike a balance between professional exigencies and personal obligations. Despite the daunting hurdles, the gratification of serving one's nation and effecting tangible change within communities renders the sacrifices eminently worthwhile. Moreover, the camaraderie and sense of purpose shared among agents create a sense of solidarity that strengthens their resolve and bolsters their resilience in the face of adversity.

The FBI's Community Impact

The FBI's imprint on communities transcends the realm of law enforcement operations, manifesting in robust engagement with local residents, educational institutions, and business entities. Agents and personnel forge bonds of trust, collaborate with stakeholders, and address community grievances. Initiatives like the Citizens Academy and the Safe Streets Task Force facilitate symbiotic collaborations between law enforcement agencies and community constituents, fostering crime prevention and outreach endeavors. By actively involving themselves in community affairs, the FBI fosters a sense of partnership and mutual responsibility, which are crucial in maintaining public safety and fostering a culture of trust between law enforcement and civilians.

Community outreach forms the cornerstone of the FBI's law enforcement paradigm, exemplified through proactive engagement, public discourse, and partnerships with community-based organizations. By fostering open channels of communication, mutual respect, and trust, the Bureau cultivates resilient, secure communities wherein every individual can thrive. Moreover, through initiatives like youth mentorship programs and educational workshops, the FBI seeks to empower individuals, particularly vulnerable populations, with the knowledge and resources needed to safeguard themselves against criminal exploitation. This proactive approach not only enhances public safety but also fosters a sense of agency and empowerment among community members.

The arduous demands intrinsic to FBI endeavors exact a toll on agents' mental and emotional equilibrium. Acknowledging the significance of mental health and well-being, the Bureau furnishes a panoply of resources and support mechanisms to aid agents and personnel in navigating stress, trauma, and burnout. Initiatives like the FBI's Employee Assistance Program furnish counseling, peer support, and wellness amenities, fostering resilience and self-care. Furthermore, by prioritizing mental health and well-being, the FBI not only enhances the effectiveness and longevity of its workforce but also sets a precedent for other organizations to follow, promoting a culture of holistic wellness and self-care in the workplace.

As we contemplate the human visage of the FBI, it becomes imperative to pay homage to the stalwart individuals who dedicate their lives to the service of their nation and the safeguarding of their communities. From acts of gallantry to instances of empathy and solidarity, the custodians behind the badge epitomize the virtues of integrity, valor, and selflessness that constitute the bedrock of the FBI's mission. Their unwavering commitment to justice and their communities serves as a beacon of inspiration, reminding us of the profound impact that individuals can have when driven by a sense of duty and a desire to make a difference.

Chapter 12 The FBI Academy

Nestled within the sprawling expanse of the Marine Corps Base Quantico, Virginia, the FBI Academy stands as an emblem of excellence in law enforcement training. Spanning 547 acres, this esteemed institution serves as the epicenter for the Federal Bureau of Investigation's preparatory endeavors, molding new recruits and seasoned professionals alike into adept guardians of justice. Boasting state-of-the-art facilities including classrooms, dormitories, a comprehensive library, dining hall, gymnasium, and meticulously crafted simulated training environments, the Academy provides a fertile ground for honing the skills and expertise requisite for safeguarding the nation's security interests.

The cornerstone of the Academy's mission lies in its steadfast commitment to preparing a cadre of elite Special Agents, Intelligence Analysts, and law enforcement personnel through a rigorous and multifaceted training regimen. The New Agent Training program, a rigorous 20-week crucible, encompasses a diverse curriculum designed to cultivate proficiency across a spectrum of essential disciplines.

Integral to this curriculum is the rigorous firearms training, where trainees undergo intensive instruction in the handling and deployment of handguns, shotguns, and rifles within dynamic, true-to-life scenarrios. Operational skills training further equips agents with the requisite prowess in defensive tactics, physical fitness, and tactical driving, ensuring their adeptness in navigating physical confrontations, maintaining peak physical conditioning, and operating vehicles under high-stress conditions. Complementing these physical aptitudes are comprehensive instruction in investigation techniques, encompassing evidence collection methodologies, adept interview techniques, and nuanced surveillance strategies—cornerstones for conducting thorough and effective investigations in a landscape characterized by traditional and modern paradigms.

Moreover, a pivotal facet of the Academy's curriculum lies in the profound emphasis on legal acumen, constitutional law, and ethics. This foundational instruction not only elucidates the boundaries within which agents must operate but also underscores the imperative of upholding the highest ethical standards—a cornerstone of the Bureau's ethos. Additionally, specialized training modules in counterterrorism and counterintelligence fortify agents with the latest strategies and tactics, empowering them to navigate the labyrinthine landscape of terrorism and espionage with acumen and foresight.
For Intelligence Analysts, the Academy's curriculum is similarly robust, with a focus on advanced analytical techniques such as data analysis, pattern recognition, and predictive modeling—essential tools for deciphering intricate datasets in support of investigative endeavors. Additionally, analysts are tutored in the craft of crafting detailed intelligence reports and delivering articulate briefings, ensuring the seamless dissemination of critical insights to decision-makers.
As a testament to its commitment to excellence, the FBI Academy extends its tutelage to seasoned law enforcement professionals through specialized programs. Leadership initiatives nurture the strategic acumen and crisis management prowess of mid-to-senior level officials, while advanced tactical training modules cater to specialized units, focusing on nuanced aspects such as hostage rescue and high-risk arrest operations. In acknowledgment of the burgeoning significance of cybersecurity, the Academy offers courses in cyber threat detection, digital forensics, and information security, equipping agents and analysts alike to navigate the complexities of the digital frontier.
Central to the Academy's ethos is an unwavering dedication to fostering a culture of continuous learning and professional development. Agents

and analysts are enjoined to partake in ongoing education endeavors, from attending refresher courses to engaging in advanced training, ensuring that the Bureau maintains a cadre of highly skilled and adaptive professionals poised to confront the exigencies of contemporary law enforcement and national security.

In summation, the FBI Academy stands as an unparalleled crucible wherein the Bureau's personnel are forged into paragons of integrity, proficiency, and unwavering resolve. Through its meticulous training programs and steadfast commitment to excellence, the Academy ensures that agents and analysts emerge primed to confront the myriad challenges of safeguarding the nation's security interests with unparalleled efficacy and discernment.

The FBI places a paramount emphasis on community engagement and education as integral components of its comprehensive cybersecurity strategy. Recognizing that effective cybersecurity extends beyond technological solutions and policy enforcement, the FBI aims to foster a well-informed public to create a collective defense against cyber threats. By educating individuals, businesses, and communities, the agency transforms them into active participants in safeguarding the digital realm.

Central to the FBI's efforts is the goal of raising awareness about various cyber threats, such as phishing, identity theft, and ransomware. Through targeted awareness campaigns, the FBI demystifies these threats, helping people understand the methods used by cybercriminals and the potential consequences of cyber attacks. This awareness is crucial in empowering the public to recognize and respond to cyber threats proactively.

Educational initiatives form the backbone of the FBI's community engagement strategy. The agency conducts a range of programs tailored to different audiences, including students, educators, parents, and senior citizens. Workshops, seminars, and webinars cover topics like safe online behavior, recognizing suspicious activities, and protecting personal information. By reaching out to diverse demographic groups, the FBI ensures that everyone, from the young to the elderly, is equipped with the knowledge needed to navigate the digital world safely.

School partnerships are another key strategy. By collaborating with educational institutions, the FBI integrates cybersecurity curricula and resources into school programs, teaching students about cyber hygiene and inspiring them to consider careers in cybersecurity. This approach not only enhances student awareness but also addresses the growing demand for skilled cybersecurity professionals.

The FBI also leverages public service announcements (PSAs) across various media platforms to highlight current cyber threats and provide safety tips. These PSAs are broadcast on television, radio, and social media, ensuring wide reach and accessibility. Regularly updated content reflects the evolving nature of cyber threats, keeping the public informed about the latest dangers and protective measures.

Promoting best practices is a continuous effort. The FBI's online presence, through its website and social media channels, offers a wealth of resources, including guides, checklists, and interactive tools that help individuals and organizations assess their cybersecurity posture and implement effective measures. Community outreach efforts, facilitated by FBI field offices, involve agents participating in local events, town hall meetings, and community groups to provide firsthand information and support. These engagements foster trust and collaboration, creating a united front against cybercrime.

Collaborations with private sector partners enhance the FBI's outreach. By working with businesses, industry associations, and non-profit organizations, the FBI leverages their networks and expertise to amplify its message and reach a broader audience. Joint initiatives, such as co-hosted webinars and shared resources, strengthen collective cybersecurity efforts.

The impact of the FBI's commitment to community engagement and education is evident in the increased public awareness and proactive measures taken by individuals and organizations to protect their digital environments. Looking ahead, the FBI plans to expand its educational initiatives, using emerging technologies like virtual reality and interactive simulations for immersive learning experiences. The agency will continue to adapt its strategies to address new and emerging cyber threats, ensuring the public remains well-informed and resilient.

In conclusion, community engagement and education are vital to the FBI's holistic approach to cybersecurity. By empowering the public with knowledge and resources, the FBI not only enhances individual and collective security but also builds a stronger, more resilient digital society.

Chapter 13: The FBI's Role in Counterterrorism

FBI's Role in Preventing Terrorism

Counterterrorism is a core mission of the FBI, requiring vigilance, coordination, and strategic partnerships to prevent terrorist attacks, dismantle extremist networks, and hold perpetrators accountable. This chapter delves into the FBI's pivotal role in counterterrorism, examining its investigative methodologies, successes, challenges, and the ever-evolving landscape of terrorist threats.

Counterterrorism encompasses a spectrum of measures aimed at thwarting terrorist plots, disrupting extremist networks, and safeguarding civilians and critical infrastructure. The FBI assumes a central position in domestic counterterrorism endeavors, collaborating closely with federal, state, local, and international counterparts to detect, deter, and respond to terrorist threats.

The FBI's primary objective in counterterrorism is preemptive action—to prevent attacks before they materialize. This proactive stance involves intelligence gathering, investigative pursuits, and disruption tactics, such as surveillance and infiltration. By identifying and neutralizing threats at their inception, the FBI strives to uphold national security and public safety.

Employing a multifaceted investigative approach, the FBI harnesses human intelligence, technical surveillance, and analytical capabilities to combat terrorism. Agents and analysts deploy various tools, including interviews, surveillance techniques, and forensic analysis, to unearth terrorist plots and amass evidence for prosecution. Moreover, the Bureau engages in community outreach initiatives targeting at-risk populations to thwart radicalization and dissuade individuals from affiliating with terrorist organizations.

Effective counterterrorism hinges on collaboration across governmental tiers and international borders. The FBI engages in seamless coordination with entities such as the Department of Homeland Security and foreign intelligence services to share intelligence, synchronize operations, and counter threats. Joint task forces, fusion centers, and international partnerships amplify the Bureau's capacity to detect and disrupt terrorist activities.

The terrorist threat landscape is dynamic, characterized by evolving tactics and technological exploitation. Terrorist entities adapt their strategies, leverage technological advancements, and exploit cyberspace vulnerabilities to orchestrate attacks. Lone actors, driven by extremist ideologies, pose a mounting menace, leveraging social media and encrypted communications for radicalization and mobilization. Addressing these emergent threats mandates agility, innovation, and interagency collaboration.

A significant case study in the FBI's counterterrorism efforts is the protracted War on Terror post-9/11. This epoch saw the genesis of Joint Terrorism Task Forces (JTTFs) and an overhaul of the Bureau's priorities. Over two decades, extensive intelligence gathering, surveillance, and law enforcement operations targeted terrorist networks, culminating in the dismantling of al-Qaeda's core leadership and the disruption of plots.

However, the FBI's counterterrorism endeavors have encountered scrutiny, particularly regarding civil liberties, privacy rights, and investigative methodologies. Debates persist regarding the efficacy and ethical implications of counterterrorism measures such as watchlists and surveillance programs.

Looking forward, the FBI must evolve to confront emerging threats. This necessitates investments in technology, bolstering analytical capacities, and fortifying partnerships with vulnerable communities. By adopting a holistic, risk-based approach, the FBI can mitigate threats, safeguard against attacks, and preserve the rule of law and civil liberties in the pursuit of national security

The FBI Albuquerque Division's Operational Medicine (OpMed) personnel partner with the Air Force Pararescue (PJ) Program and the FBI's School of Operational Medicine for a wilderness medicine course. Special agent medics provide care in high-stress tactical situations.

Chapter 14: Evolution of the FBI and Computer Science

The Federal Bureau of Investigation (FBI) has long been at the forefront of law enforcement, tackling a wide array of complex crimes. As technology has evolved, so too have the methods and tools required to combat criminal activities. In recent years, the collaboration between the FBI and computer scientists has become increasingly vital in addressing modern threats, from cybercrime to digital espionage. This article explores the dynamic partnership between the FBI and computer science experts, highlighting key developments and the profound impact of this alliance on contemporary law enforcement.

The digital revolution has transformed every aspect of society, including the nature of crime. Traditional forms of criminal activity have migrated to digital platforms, creating new challenges for law enforcement agencies worldwide. Cybercrime, including hacking, identity theft, and ransomware attacks, has proliferated, posing significant risks to individuals, corporations, and national security. To address these sophisticated threats, the FBI has turned to the expertise of computer scientists.

The Role of Computer Scientists in the FBI

Computer scientists bring a wealth of knowledge and technical skills to the FBI, aiding in the development of advanced tools and techniques for investigating and preventing cybercrimes. Their contributions can be broadly categorized into several key areas:

1. Cyber Forensics: Computer scientists assist the FBI in analyzing digital evidence, tracing cyberattacks to their sources, and recovering data that may have been encrypted or deleted. Their expertise is crucial in piecing together the digital footprints left by cybercriminals.

2. Cryptography: With the widespread use of encryption to protect data, the FBI relies on cryptographers to decrypt information and gain access to critical evidence. This requires a deep understanding of encryption algorithms and the ability to develop methods for breaking these codes when legally authorized.

3. Malware Analysis: Computer scientists specializing in malware analysis help the FBI identify, dissect, and neutralize malicious software. By understanding how malware operates, they can develop strategies to protect systems and networks from future attacks.

4. Artificial Intelligence and Machine Learning: The application of AI and machine learning has revolutionized many aspects of cyber investigations. These technologies enable the FBI to analyze vast amounts of data, detect patterns, and predict potential threats more efficiently than ever before.

5. Network Security: Protecting the FBI's own digital infrastructure is paramount. Computer scientists work to ensure that the Bureau's systems are secure from external threats, implementing robust security measures and constantly monitoring for vulnerabilities.

One of the most significant collaborations between the FBI and computer scientists has been the development of the National Cyber Investigative Joint Task Force (NCIJTF). This multi-agency task force leverages the expertise of computer scientists from various government entities to coordinate responses to cyber threats. The NCIJTF has been instrumental in disrupting numerous cybercriminal operations and enhancing national cybersecurity.

Another groundbreaking initiative is the FBI's partnership with academic institutions. Through programs such as the Cyber Internship Program, the Bureau recruits top computer science students and professionals, providing them with opportunities to work on real-world cyber investigations. This not only bolsters the FBI's capabilities but also fosters a new generation of cybercrime fighters.

The FBI has also invested heavily in research and development, working closely with private sector companies and research institutions to stay ahead of emerging threats. Projects focusing on quantum computing, advanced encryption techniques, and biometric security are just a few examples of how the FBI is preparing for the future of law enforcement.

While the collaboration between the FBI and computer scientists has yielded significant advancements, it also raises important ethical and legal questions. Balancing the need for security with the protection of individual privacy rights is a constant challenge. The use of advanced surveillance technologies and the potential for abuse necessitate stringent oversight and clear guidelines to ensure that the FBI's actions are both legal and ethical.

Additionally, the rapid pace of technological change means that the FBI must continually adapt and evolve. Staying ahead of cybercriminals requires ongoing investment in training, research, and technology. The Bureau must also foster a culture of innovation, encouraging its agents and analysts to think creatively and embrace new approaches.

As we look to the future, the partnership between the FBI and computer scientists will only become more critical. The rise of the Internet of Things (IoT), artificial intelligence, and other emerging technologies will create new opportunities for criminals and new challenges for law enforcement. By continuing to collaborate closely with computer science experts, the FBI can develop the tools and strategies needed to combat these threats effectively.

The evolution of this partnership is a testament to the importance of interdisciplinary collaboration in addressing complex societal issues. By leveraging the unique strengths of both the FBI and the computer science community, we can build a safer and more secure digital world.

The alliance between the FBI and computer scientists represents a pivotal development in the fight against modern crime. Through innovative research, advanced technology, and a commitment to ethical practices, this collaboration is transforming the landscape of law enforcement. As technology continues to evolve, the continued partnership between these two fields will be essential in safeguarding our society from the ever-changing threats of the digital age.

Chapter 15: FBI's Role in Combating Organized Crime
FBI's Approach to Combating Organized Crime

Organized crime stands as a formidable adversary, imperiling public safety, economic stability, and national security. Within this cauldron of criminality, the FBI emerges as a stalwart guardian, pivotal in thwarting organized crime syndicates, dismantling their illicit empires, and holding their kingpins accountable. This chapter delves into the annals of the FBI's storied battles against organized crime, delineating its historical struggles, contemporary methodologies, landmark cases, encountered hurdles, and prospective trajectories in the perennial war against criminal syndicates.

Organized crime embodies clandestine enterprises operating methodically, orchestrating a litany of nefarious deeds encompassing drug trafficking, extortion, money laundering, and racketeering. These malevolent syndicates engender a pervasive menace, subverting the sanctity of the rule of law, corroding institutional integrity, and perpetuating a cycle of violence and exploitation. At the helm of the FBI's mandate lies the imperative to disrupt these criminal webs, dismantle their infrastructure, and ensnare their overlords in the clutches of justice.

The FBI's foray into the fray of organized crime traces its roots to the dawn of the 20th century, epitomized by epochal clashes with legendary malefactors like Al Capone and Lucky Luciano. A watershed moment materialized with the establishment of the FBI's Organized Crime Section in the 1950s, heralding a paradigm shift in the Bureau's endeavors to destabilize and dismantle criminal syndicates. Harnessing innovative investigative methodologies, sophisticated surveillance apparatuses, and symbiotic liaisons with law enforcement cohorts, the FBI honed its sights on the leadership echelons and operational sinews of organized crime conglomerates, culminating in high-profile prosecutions and resounding convictions.

Modern Challenges and Evolutions.

Organized crime, akin to a chameleon, has metamorphosed in response to societal vicissitudes, technological advancements, and the specter of globalization. These criminal enterprises have unfurled their tentacles into new arenas, diversified their portfolios, and embraced elusive stratagems to elude the grasp of law enforcement. The advent of cybercrime, proliferation of transnational criminal syndicates, and the ubiquity of digital currencies have further complicated the battle against organized crime, impelling the FBI to recalibrate its strategies and fortify its arsenal to confront emergent threats.

The FBI orchestrates a multifaceted crusade against organized crime, marshaling an array of tactics spanning intelligence accrual, investigation, litigation, and prevention. Specialized enclaves within the FBI, such as the Organized Crime Section and the Organized Crime Drug Enforcement Task Forces (OCDETF), undertake targeted offensives against specific criminal enterprises and their illicit machinations. These bastions leverage sophisticated investigative methodologies encompassing wiretaps, undercover operations, and financial scrutiny to amass evidentiary troves and construct formidable cases against the overlords of organized crime.

The FBI's arsenal is replete with a plethora of investigative stratagems meticulously calibrated to infiltrate, destabilize, and dismantle organized crime syndicates. Undercover operatives and confidential informants ply the underbelly of criminal entities, extracting intelligence from within, while surveillance conduits and wiretaps furnish invaluable evidentiary breadcrumbs for prosecution. Financial forensics chart the circuitous routes of illicit lucre, targeting the arteries of money laundering and asset forfeiture to asphyxiate criminal enterprises financially.

Effective collaboration forms the bedrock of the FBI's campaign against organized crime, necessitating seamless orchestration across federal, state, local, and international divides. The Bureau forges symbiotic alliances with entities such as the Drug Enforcement Administration (DEA), the Bureau of Alcohol, Tobacco, Firearms and Explosives (ATF), and the Department of Homeland Security (DHS) to interweave intelligence, synchronize operations, and optimize resource utilization.

Joint task forces and intelligence-sharing conduits foster synergy, amplifying the collective riposte to the machinations of organized crime threats.

The annals of the FBI's annals are replete with tales of triumphs against organized crime, emblematic of the Bureau's mettle in dismantling criminal enterprises and ensnaring their overlords in the web of justice. Episodic sagas such as the decimation of the Gambino crime family and the evisceration of international drug trafficking syndicates serve as testament to the efficacy of the FBI's investigative prowess and collaborative ventures. These triumphs have dealt grievous blows to nefarious enterprises, dismantling their malevolent edifices and fortifying communities against the deleterious impacts of organized crime.

Despite accolades, the FBI grapples with a panoply of challenges in its campaign against organized crime, encompassing the metastasizing tide of digital technologies, the encroaching specter of globalized criminal syndicates, and the tenacity of entrenched criminal networks. Confronting these hurdles necessitates unflagging investment in technological apparatuses, fortification of intelligence conduits, and deepened collaboration with domestic and international partners. The Bureau accords primacy to preventive endeavors, targeting the root substrata of organized crime through outreach initiatives, educational endeavors, and awareness campaigns.
Looking ahead, the FBI remains resolute in its crusade against organized crime, poised to surmount emergent threats through innovation, collaboration, and strategic partnerships. Future trajectories will hinge upon the judicious leveraging of data analytics, artificial intelligence, and sundry advanced technologies to invigorate investigative capacities and undermine the operational footholds of criminal syndicates. By maintaining a vigilant vigil and adapting to the fluid contours of the criminal landscape, the FBI aspires to shield communities from the predations of organized crime and fortify the edifice of justice and civil order.

Chapter 16: Special Agent Witness Protection
FBI's Role in Witness Protection

Witness protection programs stand as bastions of security, shielding individuals who courageously step forward to offer vital testimony in criminal proceedings. This chapter embarks on an expedition through the labyrinthine corridors of the FBI's involvement in witness protection, unraveling its genesis, the intricate enrollment process, the gamut of protective measures deployed, challenges encountered, and glimpses into the vista of witness protection programs yet to unfold.

The genesis of witness protection programs traces back to the inception of the federal Witness Security Program in the 1960s, conceived to shelter witnesses entangled in organized crime cases. Over epochs, witness protection programs burgeoned, extending their protective aegis to encompass a kaleidoscope of criminal contexts spanning terrorism, drug trade, and gang violence. These programs metamorphosed into comprehensive fortresses, offering not just refuge but also relocation and support to witnesses and their kin.

The FBI stands as the fulcrum of witness protection, orchestrating the intricate ballet of enrollment, relocation, and perpetual security for protected witnesses. Nestled within the bosom of witness protection units, FBI's special agents orchestrate a symphony of collaboration with prosecutors, law enforcement agencies, and sundry stakeholders to calibrate bespoke protection plans. Armed with a panoply of intelligence, surveillance, and security acumen, the FBI ensconces itself as the vanguard of witness protection endeavors.

The odyssey of enrolling in witness protection unfurls with a meticulous appraisal of the witness's milieu, gauging the threat quotient posed by defendants and their acolytes. Once deemed worthy of the protective shroud, witnesses are summoned to unfurl a tapestry of detailed statements, undergo scrutinous background perusal, and acquiesce to the labyrinthine litany of program strictures. Embraced within the chrysalis of witness protection, witnesses and their kin are endowed with new identities, documentation, and financial sustenance to navigate the labyrinth of relocation and integration into alien environs.

Witness protection programs erect an impenetrable bastion of security, harnessing a pantheon of protection measures and security protocols to forestall the specter of harm. From fortified domiciles to cloistered conveyance, physical security measures bolster the citadel of safety, while operational strictures such as communication curbs and access embargo to personal data shield the sanctum of anonymity. A retinue of specialized sentinels and law enforcement officers vigilantly guard protected witnesses, ready to proffer swift responses to any encroachment or breach of security. Witness protection programs confront a menagerie of challenges and risks, navigating the labyrinth of perpetual secrecy, the specter of tampering and intimidation, and the emotional toll exacted on witnesses and their clans. Striking the equipoise between the exigencies of protection and the yearnings for autonomy demands deft choreography, fostering a crucible of coordination and communication between program custodians and participants.

Amidst the labyrinth of challenges, witness protection programs unfurl a tapestry of triumphs, fashioning convictions, disentangling criminal syndicates, and enfolding witnesses and their clans within the embrace of safety. Testimonials from the sanctum of protected witnesses resonate with the chorus of salvation, underscoring the life-preserving import of witness protection and the indelible contributions of those who dare to tread the path of righteousness. These narratives bespeak the resonance of witness protection in upholding the tapestry of justice and affording solace to victims of crime.

The vista of witness protection looms large with prospects of innovation, collaboration, and adaptation to burgeoning threats and exigencies. The imminence of technological frontiers, epitomized by biometric markers and digital bastions, holds the promise of fortifying the ramparts of witness protection programs. Collaboration with international allies and private entities may broaden the ambit of witness protection programs. Collaboration with international allies and private entities may broaden the ambit of witness protection endeavors, forging a global consortium of safety and sanctuary. At the heart of this epochal voyage lies an unwavering commitment to shielding witnesses and safeguarding the sanctity of the criminal justice edifice.

(https://www.fbi.gov/services/witness-protection).

Chapter 17: Special Agent: Top Secret Cases

Top secret cases represent the apex of sensitivity and urgency within the FBI's investigative portfolio. These cases delve into matters of national security, espionage, terrorism, and other covert activities that threaten the United States' interests and safety. Special agents assigned to these high-stakes investigations operate under the strictest levels of confidentiality and scrutiny, often collaborating with other federal agencies, intelligence community partners, and international allies to safeguard the nation.

Top secret cases span a vast array of threats and activities, from foreign espionage operations and cyber attacks to terrorist plots and the proliferation of weapons of mass destruction. These investigations demand agents with specialized skills in intelligence analysis, surveillance techniques, and interagency cooperation. Navigating complex legal, diplomatic, and geopolitical landscapes, these agents protect sensitive information and sources, ensuring national security is upheld.

The FBI leads the charge in addressing top secret threats to national security. Specialized units within the Bureau, including those focused on counterintelligence, counterterrorism, and cyber investigations, conduct thorough investigations to gather intelligence and disrupt hostile actions against the United States. These efforts often extend beyond domestic borders, involving coordination with foreign intelligence counterparts and international security agencies.

Notable Top Secret Cases

1. Foreign Espionage: Aldrich Ames
From 1985 to 1994, Aldrich Ames, a CIA officer, spied for the Soviet Union and later Russia, compromising numerous CIA operations and leading to the exposure and deaths of several U.S. intelligence assets. This case remains one of the most damaging espionage breaches in U.S. history.

- Date: 1985-1994
- Impact: Significant compromise of CIA operations and intelligence sources, resulting in multiple fatalities among U.S. assets.

2. Cyber Attacks: Operation Crossfire Hurricane

The 2016 Russian interference in the U.S. presidential election, known as «Operation Crossfire Hurricane,» involved extensive efforts by Russian operatives to manipulate public opinion and undermine confidence in the electoral process.

- Date: 2016
- Impact: Uncovered widespread Russian interference, leading to indictments and sanctions against individuals and entities involved.

3. Terrorist Plots: The 9/11 PENTTBOM Investigation

Following the September 11, 2001, terrorist attacks, the FBI's PENTTBOM investigation sought to identify and dismantle the terrorist network responsible for the attacks on the World Trade Center and the Pentagon.

- Date: September 11, 2001
- Impact: Led to the identification, capture, and prosecution of key al-Qaeda operatives involved in the attacks.

4. Nuclear Proliferation: The A.Q. Khan Network

The investigation into the A.Q. Khan network focused on the illicit transfer of nuclear technology and materials to countries like Iran, North Korea, and Libya, significantly impacting global nuclear non-proliferation efforts.

- Date: 1972-2004
- Impact: Contributed to dismantling the network and preventing the spread of nuclear weapons technology.

Challenges and Risks in Top Secret Investigations

Conducting top secret investigations involves significant challenges and risks:

1. Operational Security: Maintaining the secrecy and integrity of operations and protecting sensitive information from leaks or unauthorized access.

2. Threats to Agents: Facing potential threats from hostile actors aiming to obstruct investigations, compromise sources, or retaliate against agents.

3. Legal Constraints: Balancing the need for thorough investigation with adherence to legal and constitutional principles, particularly regarding surveillance and intelligence gathering.

4. Diplomatic Sensitivities: Managing international relations and diplomatic implications while investigating activities with global repercussions.

Handling Classified Information

Agents involved in top secret investigations receive extensive training and security clearances to handle classified information. They adhere to strict protocols for accessing, storing, and disseminating classified material, ensuring its protection against unauthorized access or disclosure. Violations of these protocols can lead to severe consequences, including criminal prosecution and loss of security clearance.

Successes and Impact

The FBI's top secret investigations have yielded significant successes, safeguarding national security, disrupting hostile activities, and protecting critical infrastructure. The intelligence gathered informs policymakers, supports diplomatic efforts, and enhances the nation's ability to respond to emerging threats. The dedication and expertise of special agents in these investigations are crucial to the FBI's mission of protecting the United States.

Ethical Considerations

Ethical considerations are paramount in top secret investigations. Agents must navigate the tension between national security and civil liberties, privacy rights, and the rule of law. Upholding democratic values, transparency, accountability, and respect for constitutional principles is essential in conducting these investigations.

The Future of Top Secret Investigations

The landscape of top secret investigations is continually evolving with technological advancements, emerging threats, and shifting geopolitical dynamics. Special agents will need to adapt to challenges such as cyber warfare, disinformation campaigns, and hybrid threats, while maintaining vigilance against traditional espionage and terrorism. Collaboration with domestic and international partners will remain critical in addressing top secret threats and protecting national security interests.

Chapter 18: Future Projects for the FBI Technological Innovations

The FBI is gearing up to exploit the immense potential of artificial intelligence (AI) and machine learning (ML) algorithms to manage the vast amounts of data it accumulates. By deploying these advanced tools, the Bureau aims to identify intricate patterns, uncover hidden correlations, and detect emerging threats within the digital landscape. Integrating AI-driven solutions into its investigative processes is expected to enhance the FBI's ability to anticipate and address risks with speed and precision. For example, AI can be utilized to analyze large datasets from social media and other digital platforms to identify potential terrorist activities or cyber threats before they materialize.

With the constant threat of cyber-attacks, the FBI is committed to strengthening its cybersecurity measures. By adopting state-of-the-art cybersecurity technologies, the Bureau aims to build a robust defense system around critical infrastructure, protecting it from cybercrime. The FBI plans to employ advanced tools for digital forensics, threat intelligence, and network security to effectively combat cyber threats. Innovations such as blockchain for secure data transactions and quantum encryption for impenetrable communications are on the horizon.

Biometric technologies, including facial recognition and fingerprint analysis, are set to play a pivotal role in the FBI's future operations. These technologies will enhance the Bureau's ability to accurately identify individuals, thereby improving the effectiveness of criminal investigations. The FBI's Next Generation Identification (NGI) system, which integrates biometric data from various sources, exemplifies the Bureau's commitment to leveraging biometrics for improved law enforcement capabilities.

The persistent threat of terrorism requires a comprehensive and adaptive approach. The FBI is focused on enhancing its counterterrorism strategies by fostering greater collaboration among federal, state, and local agencies, as well as international partners. The Bureau is also investing in advanced surveillance technologies and data analytics to preempt and neutralize terrorist activities. Community engagement and intelligence gathering are crucial components of this strategy, helping to identify and disrupt radicalization efforts at their inception.

In the digital age, the FBI stands as a crucial defender against cybercrime. The Bureau is expanding its cyber capabilities by forming strategic partnerships with leading technology companies and academic institutions. These collaborations aim to develop innovative tools for tracking and prosecuting cybercriminals. The FBI's Cyber Division is at the forefront of these efforts, utilizing cutting-edge digital forensics to trace cyberattacks back to their source and bring perpetrators to justice.

Transnational criminal organizations pose a significant challenge in a globalized world. The FBI is committed to dismantling these networks through coordinated efforts with international law enforcement agencies. By sharing intelligence and resources, the Bureau aims to disrupt the operations of criminal syndicates involved in activities such as human trafficking, drug smuggling, and financial fraud. Initiatives like the FBI's International Operations Division underscore the importance of global cooperation in combating transnational crime.

Building trust and cooperation with local communities is essential for effective law enforcement. The FBI is dedicated to fostering strong relationships with diverse communities through outreach programs that promote mutual understanding and collaboration. These efforts aim to empower communities, enhance public safety, and create a sense of shared responsibility in the fight against crime .

To improve information sharing and coordination, the FBI is establishing intelligence fusion centers that bring together federal, state, and local law enforcement agencies. These centers facilitate the rapid exchange of intelligence, enabling a unified response to emerging threats. By pooling expertise and resources, the fusion centers enhance the overall effectiveness of law enforcement operations .

Preventing crime before it occurs is a key focus for the FBI. The Bureau is implementing intervention programs aimed at at-risk individuals and communities, providing mentorship, support, and access to social services. These programs are designed to address the root causes of criminal behavior, offering alternatives that steer individuals away from crime and towards positive contributions to society .

As the FBI navigates the challenges of the future, these projects represent its commitment to innovation, strategic advancement, and collaboration. By leveraging cutting-edge technologies, enhancing operational initiatives, and fostering partnerships, the Bureau is dedicated to protecting the American public and upholding the rule of law.

Biometric Technology Center (BTC) on the campus of the Criminal Justice Information Services Division in Clarksburg, West Virginia. The center, opened in 2015, is an enhancement of the ongoing collaboration between the FBI's Biometric Center of Excellence and the Department of Defense's Forensics and Biometrics Agency and will encourage even more joint biometric investigations, along with additional research and development.

Chapter 19: Inside the of Mind an FBI Agent

Delving into the mindset of an FBI agent offers insights into the unique blend of skills, qualities, and experiences that shape their approach to investigative work. This chapter provides a glimpse into the world of an FBI agent, exploring their motivations, mindset, challenges, and strategies for success, accompanied by a compelling anecdote from the field.

FBI agents are driven by a deep sense of duty, patriotism, and a desire to serve and protect their country. Their commitment to upholding the rule of law, safeguarding national security, and seeking justice for victims of crime fuels their dedication to the job. Many agents are drawn to the FBI by a sense of purpose and the opportunity to make a meaningful difference in the world.

FBI agents possess a resilient mindset characterized by adaptability, perseverance, and mental toughness. They are trained to thrive in high-pressure environments, navigate uncertainty, and overcome obstacles with determination and resourcefulness. The ability to maintain focus, stay calm under pressure, and remain vigilant in the face of danger is essential for success in the field.

Skills and Qualities:

FBI agents possess a diverse set of skills and qualities that enable them to excel in their roles:

Investigative Skills: Agents are trained in advanced investigative techniques, including evidence collection, surveillance, and interrogation. They have a keen eye for detail, analytical thinking skills, and the ability to connect seemingly unrelated pieces of information to uncover the truth.

Communication Skills: Effective communication is essential for building rapport with witnesses, eliciting information from suspects, and collaborating with colleagues and partners. Agents must be adept at both verbal and written communication, able to articulate complex ideas clearly and persuasively.

Adaptability: The nature of FBI work is unpredictable, requiring agents to adapt quickly to changing circumstances, environments, and threats. Flexibility, creativity, and the ability to think on their feet are critical for navigating dynamic situations and achieving successful outcomes.

Ethical Integrity: Upholding the highest ethical standards is paramount for FBI agents, who must adhere to strict codes of conduct and respect constitutional rights in the pursuit of justice. Integrity, honesty, and a commitment to fairness guide their actions and decision-making processes.

Anecdote: «The Undercover Operation»

One FBI agent, let's call him Agent Smith, was assigned to an undercover operation targeting a notorious drug trafficking organization operating in a major city. Posing as a low-level criminal looking to expand his network, Agent Smith infiltrated the organization and gained the trust of its leaders over several months of covert surveillance and intelligence gathering.

As the operation progressed, Agent Smith found himself in increasingly dangerous situations, facing threats from rival gangs, betrayals from within the organization, and the constant risk of his cover being blown. Despite the risks, Agent Smith remained focused on his mission, relying on his training, instincts, and the support of his fellow agents to navigate the treacherous underworld of organized crime.

Finally, after months of painstaking investigation, Agent Smith and his team were able to gather enough evidence to dismantle the drug trafficking ring and bring its leaders to justice. The operation was a success, but it came at a cost — Agent Smith had put his life on the line to protect his community and uphold the rule of law.

Challenges and Rewards

Working as an FBI agent presents numerous challenges, including:

- **Risk of Danger**: Agents often operate in high-risk environments, facing potential danger from armed suspects, violent criminals, and hazardous situations.

- **Emotional Toll**: Investigating crimes, particularly those involving violence or exploitation, can take an emotional toll on agents, requiring resilience and self-care to cope with the stress and trauma.

- **Work-Life Balance**:The demands of FBI work, including long hours, travel, and unpredictable schedules, can strain personal relationships and impact agents' work-life balance.

Despite these challenges, the rewards of FBI work are significant:

- **Sense of Purpose**: Making a positive impact on society and protecting the public gives agents a profound sense of purpose and fulfillment.
- Professional Development: The FBI offers extensive training, career advancement opportunities, and exposure to diverse investigative assignments, allowing agents to continually develop their skills and expertise.

- **Camaraderie and Support**: Agents form close bonds with their colleagues, sharing a sense of camaraderie, teamwork, and mutual support that fosters a strong organizational culture.

To succeed as an FBI agent, individuals must:

- **Embrace Continuous Learning**: Stay informed about emerging threats, new technologies, and evolving investigative techniques through ongoing training and professional development.

- **Build Relationships**: Cultivate strong relationships with colleagues, partners, and communities to foster collaboration, trust, and information sharing.

- **Stay Grounded**: Maintain a healthy work-life balance, prioritize self-care, and seek support from peers and mentors to manage stress and maintain resilience.

The mindset of an FBI agent is characterized by dedication, resilience, and a commitment to upholding the values of the Bureau. Through rigorous training, diverse experiences, and a sense of purpose, agents embody the principles of justice, integrity, and service that define the FBI's mission to protect and defend the United States.

PART II

Chapter 1: Interview

Let's dive deeper into the details and provide more comprehensive insights and developments about the work of an FBI agent with this interview of Sarah M.

Interviewer: Thank you for joining us today Sarah M. Can you start by introducing yourself and telling us a bit about your role at the FBI?

FBI Agent: Of course. My name is Special Agent Sarah M., and I've been with the FBI for over 10 years. I currently work in the Cyber Crimes Division, where we investigate various forms of cybercrime, including hacking, cyber terrorism, and online fraud.

Interviewer: That sounds fascinating. What drew you to a career with the FBI?

FBI Agent : I've always been passionate about serving my community and protecting people. The FBI's mission to uphold and enforce the laws of the United States while protecting and defending against terrorist and foreign intelligence threats resonated deeply with me. Additionally, my background in computer science made the Cyber Crimes Division a perfect fit.

Interviewer: Can you describe a typical day on the job?

FBI Agent: Every day is different, which is one of the things I love about my job. A typical day might involve analyzing data from a cyberattack, coordinating with other agencies, interviewing witnesses or suspects, and preparing reports. We also spend a significant amount of time training and staying updated on the latest cyber threats and technologies.

Interviewer: What has been one of the most challenging cases you've worked on?

FBI Agent : One of the most challenging cases involved a complex ransomware attack on a major healthcare provider. The attackers had encrypted sensitive patient data and were demanding a substantial ransom. We had to work around the clock to trace the source of the attack, mitigate the damage, and eventually bring the perpetrators to justice. It required a coordinated effort across multiple divisions and agencies, both domestic and international.

Interviewer: Could you elaborate on the process of investigating such a case?

FBI Agent : Certainly. When we receive a report of a cyberattack, our first step is to secure the affected systems to prevent further damage. We work closely with the victim organization to understand the scope of the attack and identify any potential vulnerabilities that were exploited. Our technical experts then analyze the malware used in the attack, looking for unique signatures or coding patterns that can help trace it back to the perpetrators. We also collaborate with international law enforcement agencies and cybersecurity firms to share information and resources. Once we have enough evidence, we proceed to apprehend the suspects and work with prosecutors to build a solid case against them.

Interviewer: What has been the impact of technological advancements on your work?

FBI Agent : Technological advancements have been a double-edged sword. On one hand, they have provided us with sophisticated tools for tracking and combating cyber threats. On the other hand, they have also given criminals more advanced methods to perpetrate their crimes. For instance, the rise of cryptocurrencies has made it easier for criminals to conduct transactions anonymously. However, we've also developed advanced forensic techniques to track these transactions and uncover their origins. Staying ahead of these developments requires continuous learning and adaptation.

Interviewer: How do you stay current with the latest cyber threats and technologies?

FBI Agent : Continuous education and training are essential in this field. The FBI provides ongoing training programs, and we also attend conferences and workshops on cybersecurity. Additionally, we maintain strong partnerships with academic institutions, private sector companies, and other government agencies. These collaborations help us stay informed about emerging threats and innovative solutions. We also subscribe to cybersecurity journals and participate in online forums where professionals share insights and best practices.

Interviewer: What skills are essential for someone in your line of work?

FBI Agent : Critical thinking and problem-solving skills are crucial. You need to be able to analyze complex data and situations quickly and accurately. Technical skills, especially in computer science and cybersecurity, are also essential. Additionally, strong communication skills are important because we often work in teams and need to convey complex information clearly. Investigative skills, such as interviewing techniques and attention to detail, are also vital. Lastly, resilience and stress management are important, given the high-pressure nature of our work.

Interviewer: How do you handle the stress and pressure that comes with your job?

FBI Agent: It's definitely a demanding job, but we have a strong support system within the FBI. Regular physical training helps, as does ensuring I take time for myself and my family. It's also vital to stay focused on the mission and the positive impact our work has on society. The FBI offers resources such as counseling services and stress management workshops. Personally, I find that hobbies like hiking and reading help me unwind and maintain a healthy work-life balance.

Interviewer: Can you share any memorable moments or highlights from your career?

FBI Agent: One memorable moment was when we successfully thwarted a large-scale cyber attack on a financial institution. The attack had the potential to disrupt major financial transactions across the country. Our team worked tirelessly for days, and the sense of accomplishment and relief when we neutralized the threat was immense. Another highlight was participating in an international operation to dismantle a major cybercrime syndicate. The operation involved coordination with agencies from multiple countries and resulted in the arrest of key figures responsible for numerous cyber attacks worldwide.

Interviewer: What advice would you give to someone aspiring to join the FBI?

FBI Agent Johnson: Be prepared for a rigorous selection process and make sure you have a strong educational and professional background. Integrity, dedication, and a commitment to public service are essential. Also, never stop learning and improving your skills. The threats we face are constantly evolving, and we need to be able to adapt and stay ahead. It's also important to develop a strong support network and to take care of your physical and mental health. Lastly, be patient and persistent. The path to becoming an FBI agent can be long and challenging, but it's incredibly rewarding.

Interviewer: you were at FBI Academy Can you give us an overview of what the training entails?

FBI Agent: Absolutely. The FBI Academy is where all special agents receive their initial training. The program is about 20 weeks long and is designed to prepare new agents for the diverse challenges they'll face in the field. The training includes a mix of academic coursework, practical exercises, and physical fitness training. Recruits are trained in everything from law and investigative techniques to firearms proficiency and defensive tactics.

Interviewer: Can you elaborate on the academic coursework at the Academy?

FBI Agent: Certainly. The academic portion of the training covers a wide range of subjects essential for an FBI agent. This includes courses on federal law, constitutional law, investigative procedures, forensics, ethics, and cybersecurity. Recruits also study behavioral science to better understand criminal behavior and learn techniques for interviewing and interrogation. These courses provide the foundational knowledge that agents need to effectively conduct investigations and uphold the law.

Interviewer: What kind of practical exercises do recruits undergo?

FBI Agent: Practical exercises are a critical component of the training. Recruits participate in simulated scenarios that mimic real-life situations they might encounter as agents. These scenarios can include everything from executing search warrants and arresting suspects to handling hostage situations and conducting surveillance operations. These exercises are designed to test recruits' problem-solving skills, teamwork, and ability to perform under pressure. Additionally, there are specific modules focused on cybercrime, counterterrorism, and counterintelligence, reflecting the diverse nature of the FBI's work.

Interviewer: Physical fitness seems to be a big part of the training. Can you tell us more about that?

FBI Agent: Physical fitness is indeed a significant part of the training at the FBI Academy. Agents need to be physically prepared for the demands of the job, which can be quite strenuous. Recruits undergo rigorous physical training that includes running, strength training, and agi-

agility exercises. There's also a focus on defensive tactics, where recruits learn how to safely subdue suspects and protect themselves and others. We have specific fitness benchmarks that all recruits must meet to graduate from the Academy.

Interviewer: What are some of the key qualities and skills the FBI looks for in new agents?

FBI Agent: The FBI looks for a combination of qualities and skills in new agents. Integrity and strong ethical standards are paramount, as agents are entrusted with significant responsibilities. Critical thinking and problem-solving skills are also crucial, as agents often face complex and rapidly evolving situations. Strong communication skills are essential for interviewing witnesses, writing reports, and testifying in court. Physical fitness, resilience, and the ability to work well under pressure are also important. Lastly, a commitment to continuous learning and adaptability is vital, given the constantly changing nature of crime and law enforcement.

Interviewer: Can you share any memorable moments or challenges you've faced while training new recruits?

FBI Agent: One memorable moment was watching a recruit who initially struggled with the physical fitness requirements push through and ultimately meet all the benchmarks. It was a testament to their determination and resilience. On the challenging side, ensuring that all recruits fully grasp the seriousness and complexity of their future roles can be difficult. We use real-life case studies and bring in experienced agents to speak to recruits, which helps bridge the gap between theory and practice. Seeing recruits grow and develop into capable agents is incredibly rewarding.

Interviewer: How does the training at the Academy evolve to keep up with new threats and technologies?

FBI Agent: The training at the Academy is continuously updated to address new threats and incorporate the latest technologies. We work closely with various divisions within the FBI to identify emerging trends in crime and law enforcement. For example, as cybercrime has become more prevalent, we've significantly expanded our cybersecurity training. We also incorporate lessons learned from recent cases and adapt our training scenarios accordingly. Our goal is to ensure that new agents are as prepared as possible to handle the challenges they'll face in the field.

Interviewer: What advice would you give to someone aspiring to join the FBI and go through the Academy?

FBI Agent: My advice would be to focus on developing a strong foundation of skills and knowledge. This includes pursuing higher education, gaining relevant work experience, and staying physically fit. It's also important to have a clear understanding of the FBI's mission and values, as well as a genuine commitment to public service. Be prepared for a rigorous selection process and extensive training. Finally, never underestimate the importance of resilience and adaptability. The path to becoming an FBI agent is challenging, but it's also incredibly rewarding.

Interviewer: Thank you for your time, Agent Miller. It's been enlightening to hear about the training and preparation that goes into becoming an FBI agent.

FBI Agent: Thank you. It's been a pleasure to share a bit about what we do at the Academy.

FBI Agent: Thank you. It's been a pleasure to share a bit about what we do at the Academy.

Chapter 2: Type of specialized units
Hostage Rescue Team (HRT)

Hostage Rescue Team (HRT)

The Hostage Rescue Team (HRT) is an elite tactical unit of the FBI, specializing in counterterrorism, hostage rescue, and high-risk law enforcement operations. Established in 1983, the team is primed for rapid deployment, capable of mobilizing within a mere four hours of notification to address any corner of the United States in response to terrorist activities, hostage crises, or significant criminal threats. Predominantly focused on countering terrorism and ensuring the safe liberation of captives, the HRT, as articulated by Kevin Cornelius, a former operator turned commander, holds the paramount objective of preserving lives.

While initially crafted to furnish a tactical response to terrorism, the HRT boasts an array of capabilities unparalleled in civilian law enforcement. Proficient in diverse disciplines such as helicopter insertion via fast-roping, parachuting with full gear, and executing advanced SCUBA maneuvers, operators demonstrate mastery in marksmanship, breaching techniques—including explosives—and close-quarter tactics. This expertise guarantees the HRT's ability to execute assaults with celerity, accuracy, and, if requisite, lethal force.

The primary mission of the HRT is to conduct hostage rescue operations, counterterrorism activities, and high-risk arrests. The team is trained to handle various critical situations, including:

- Hostage rescues
- Barricaded suspects
- Terrorist threats and operations
- Dignitary protection
- Crisis response

Training and Selection:

HRT members undergo rigorous training, often considered among the most intense within U.S. law enforcement. The selection process includes:
- Physical fitness assessments
- Tactical skills evaluations
- Psychological testing
- Advanced firearms training
- Specialized courses in explosives, breaching, and close-quarters combat

Operations and Deployments:

The HRT operates under the Critical Incident Response Group (CIRG) umbrella and collaborates with other federal, state, and local agencies. The team has been involved in numerous high-profile operations, including:
- The 1993 Waco Siege
- The 1996 Atlanta Olympics bombing investigation
- Various counterterrorism operations post-9/11

Critical Incident Response Group (CIRG)

The Critical Incident Response Group (CIRG) was established in 1994 to integrate various tactical and crisis management resources within the FBI. CIRG provides rapid response capabilities for a wide range of critical incidents and major events.

Divisions and Units:

CIRG comprises several specialized units and teams, each with unique functions:
1. Hostage Rescue Team (HRT): As described above, the HRT is the premier tactical unit for high-risk operations.
2. Crisis Negotiation Unit (CNU): This unit provides negotiation support during hostage situations, barricade incidents, and kidnappings.
Behavioral Analysis Unit (BAU): Experts in behavioral profiling, the BAU assists in understanding and predicting criminal behavior.
4. Operations and Support Branch: Manages logistical support, training, and operational readiness for CIRG.

Training and Resources:

CIRG personnel undergo specialized training to handle various aspects of crisis response, including:
- Incident command and control
- Advanced negotiation techniques
- Tactical operations and planning
- Coordination with local and international law enforcement

Notable Deployments:
CIRG has been instrumental in numerous critical operations, such as:
- Coordinating the FBI's response to the 9/11 attacks
- Providing crisis management support during natural disasters like Hurricane Katrina
- Managing security for major public events, including presidential inaugurations and international summits

Both the Hostage Rescue Team (HRT) and the Critical Incident Response Group (CIRG) are integral components of the FBI's capability to respond to national and international crises. The HRT specializes in tactical, high-risk operations, while CIRG encompasses a broader range of crisis management and support functions. Together, they enhance the FBI's ability to manage and resolve critical incidents effectively.

The Criminal Investigative Division (CID) of the FBI is dedicated to investigating a comprehensive spectrum of criminal activities. Its primary mission is to address organized crime, violent crime, public corruption, financial crimes, and human trafficking with unparalleled precision and expertise. To achieve this, the CID employs a multifaceted approach that includes meticulous surveillance, covert undercover operations, and advanced forensic analysis. By leveraging cutting-edge technology and strategic methodologies, the CID ensures thorough and effective investigations.

Moreover, the CID's success is significantly bolstered by its robust collaboration with other law enforcement agencies. This coordination enables the seamless sharing of intelligence, resources, and expertise, which is crucial in dismantling sophisticated criminal networks and bringing perpetrators to justice. Through these collaborative efforts, the CID not only enhances its operational capabilities but also contributes to a unified and comprehensive approach to national and international crime prevention and enforcement.

In essence, the Criminal Investigative Division stands as a formidable force within the FBI, relentlessly pursuing justice and maintaining the integrity of the legal system through its unwavering commitment to combating a wide array of criminal activities.

The Office of Private Sector (OPS) within the FBI plays a pivotal role in fortifying national security by fostering robust collaboration between the Bureau and private sector entities. This specialized unit is dedicated to enhancing information sharing, protecting critical infrastructure, and addressing a range of security issues, including cyber attacks and industrial espionage. The primary mission of the OPS is to establish and maintain effective partnerships between the FBI and the private sector, creating a unified front against emerging threats that could compromise national security. By building these alliances, the OPS ensures that both the public and private sectors are well-equipped to respond to and mitigate security risks. The OPS facilitates seamless information sharing between the FBI and its private sector partners, which is vital for identifying potential threats, understanding vulnerabilities, and developing comprehensive strategies. Protecting critical infrastructure, such as power grids, water supplies, and communication networks, is another key function of the OPS. By working closely with private sector stakeholders, the OPS implements security measures and develops contingency plans to ensure the resilience of these critical systems. Addressing cyber threats and industrial espionage, the OPS collaborates with cybersecurity experts to identify vulnerabilities, share threat intelligence, and develop defenses against cyber intrusions. Partnerships with private sector entities, spanning finance, energy, healthcare, and technology industries, bolster the OPS's efforts. These collaborations, exemplified by initiatives like the Domestic Security Alliance Council (DSAC), provide platforms for direct cooperation on homeland security matters. Through these extensive networks and partnerships, the OPS enhances the collective security posture, demonstrating the power of collaboration in safeguarding national security and economic well-being.

Chapter 3: Interview

«SWAT Team FBI» refers to the specialized SWAT (Special Weapons and Tactics) units within the Federal Bureau of Investigation. Each of the FBI's 56 field offices across the United States has its own SWAT team, composed of agents trained to handle high-risk operations. These teams are involved in a variety of missions, including counter-terrorism, hostage rescue, and operations against heavily armed criminals.

The term «SWAT agent» within the FBI refers to a member of the FBI's Special Weapons and Tactics (SWAT) teams. These are specialized units that handle high-risk operations which require enhanced tactical skills. FBI SWAT teams are part of the Critical Incident Response Group (CIRG) and are deployed to address situations such as hostage rescues, barricaded suspects, high-risk arrest and search warrants, and active shooter incidents. FBI SWAT agents undergo rigorous training to prepare for these demanding and dangerous tasks. They are trained in a variety of disciplines including tactical operations, firearms proficiency, explosive breaching, and close-quarter battle techniques. To become an FBI SWAT agent, an individual must first be an FBI Special Agent and have several years of experience with the Bureau. After this, they must pass a challenging selection process and complete extensive training programs. SWAT teams are a crucial component of the FBI's tactical response capabilities, providing a rapid and specialized response to critical situations to protect the public and ensure the safety of law enforcement personnel.

One of the elite groups within the FBI's tactical units is the Hostage Rescue Team (HRT), which often collaborates with local FBI SWAT teams on complex and dangerous missions. For instance, in a recent operation in Houston, the FBI's Hostage Rescue Team and the local SWAT team successfully rescued several hostages and arrested four suspects.

FBI SWAT teams are equipped with a range of specialized gear, including M4 carbines, Glock pistols, ballistic shields, and various armored vehicles like the Lenco BearCat and MRAPs (Mine-Resistant Ambush Protected vehicles). These teams undergo rigorous training to maintain their readiness for any situation.

Interviewer: Thank you for joining us today. Can you start by telling us a bit about yourself and your role in the FBI?

Agent Smith: Thank you for having me. My name is Agent Smith, and I've been with the FBI for over 12 years. I started as a Special Agent working on various criminal investigations before joining the SWAT team about five years ago. Currently, I'm a team leader on one of our regional SWAT teams, and our primary role is to handle high-risk operations that require specialized tactical skills.

Interviewer: What motivated you to join the SWAT team?

Agent Smith: I've always had a strong desire to serve and protect my community, and I wanted to be part of a team that handles some of the most challenging and critical situations. The camaraderie, the specialized training, and the opportunity to make a significant impact in dangerous situations were all factors that motivated me to join SWAT.

Interviewer: Can you describe the training process to become an FBI SWAT agent?

Agent Smith: Certainly. The training process is very rigorous. First, you need to be an experienced FBI Special Agent with a solid track record.

Then, you go through a selection process that tests your physical fitness, firearms proficiency, and tactical judgment. If you make it through the selection, you enter an intensive training program that includes advanced firearms training, defensive tactics, breaching techniques, close-quarter combat, and scenario-based exercises. It's physically and mentally demanding, but it prepares us for the high-stress situations we may face in the field.

Interviewer: What are some of the most challenging aspects of being a SWAT agent?

Agent Smith: One of the most challenging aspects is the unpredictability of our missions. We often deal with volatile and rapidly evolving situations, such as hostage rescues or active shooter scenarios. The physical demands are also significant, as we need to maintain peak fitness levels to perform our duties effectively. Additionally, the psychological stress can be intense, knowing that our decisions can have life-or-death consequences.

Interviewer: Can you share a memorable experience from your time on the SWAT team?

Agent Smith: There are many memorable experiences, but one that stands out is a hostage rescue operation we conducted last year. We received a call about an armed suspect who had taken hostages in a residential building. Our team had to move in quickly and decisively. Thanks to our training and coordination, we were able to safely rescue all the hostages and apprehend the suspect without any casualties. It was a moment that underscored the importance of our preparation and teamwork.

Interviewer: How do you and your team prepare for high-risk operations?

Agent Smith: Preparation is key. We conduct regular training exercises to keep our skills sharp and to ensure we can operate seamlessly as a unit. Before any operation, we gather as much intelligence as possible, create detailed tactical plans, and conduct rehearsals. Communication is crucial, so we ensure everyone understands their role and the overall strategy. We also debrief extensively after each mission to learn and improve.

Interviewer: What advice would you give to someone aspiring to join the FBI SWAT team?

Agent Smith: My advice would be to focus on building a strong foundation as an FBI Special Agent first. Gain as much experience as you can, stay physically fit, and continuously develop your tactical and decision-making skills. Perseverance and dedication are essential. It's a challenging path, but it's incredibly rewarding if you're committed to serving and protecting others.

Interviewer: Thank you for sharing your experiences and insights with us, Agent Smith. We appreciate the work you and your team do to keep us safe.

Agent Smith: Thank you. It's an honor to serve, and I appreciate the opportunity to share a bit about our work.

This fictional interview provides a glimpse into the life and responsibilities of an FBI SWAT agent, highlighting the dedication and challenges faced in this specialized role.

Certainly! Here's a focused interview with an FBI SWAT agent that delves into the recruitment process:

Interviewer: Thank you for joining us today. Can you start by telling us about the recruitment process for becoming an FBI SWAT agent?

Agent Smith: Thank you for having me. The journey to becoming an FBI SWAT agent begins with becoming a Special Agent with the FBI. The basic requirements include being a U.S. citizen, aged between 23 and 37, and holding a bachelor's degree from an accredited institution. You also need at least two years of professional work experience or one year with a qualifying advanced degree. Once these prerequisites are

You also need at least two years of professional work experience or one year with a qualifying advanced degree. Once these prerequisites are met, the application process starts.

Interviewer: What steps are involved in the application process to become a Special Agent?

Agent Smith: The application process is rigorous and multi-phased. First, you submit an online application. If it's accepted, you move on to Phase I testing, which includes a three-hour exam that assesses cognitive, behavioral, and logical reasoning skills. Passing this leads you to Phase II, which involves a writing exercise and a structured interview. Following that, you must pass the Physical Fitness Test (PFT), which includes sit-ups, a 300-meter sprint, push-ups, and a 1.5-mile run. Additionally, there's a comprehensive medical examination and a thorough background investigation, including a polygraph exam. Successful candidates then attend the FBI Academy in Quantico, Virginia, for approximately 20 weeks of intensive training.

Interviewer: Once you're an FBI Special Agent, what is the process for joining the SWAT team?

Agent Smith: After serving as an FBI Special Agent for a few years and gaining substantial field experience, you can apply to join a SWAT team. This involves a more rigorous selection process starting with a challenging SWAT Physical Fitness Test that includes advanced strength and endurance components. Candidates must also demonstrate advanced firearms proficiency.

Interviewer: Can you elaborate on the selection process and the specialized training involved?

Agent Smith: Absolutely. The selection process includes an intense assessment and selection course. This course tests candidates on various tactical skills, physical fitness, and mental resilience through stress courses, scenario-based training, and interviews. Those who pass this selection process undergo specialized SWAT training, which covers advanced tactical operations, hostage rescue, breaching techniques, close-quarters combat, and more. This training is designed to prepare agents for the high-stress and dangerous situations they might encounter in the field.

Interviewer: What kind of ongoing training do SWAT agents participate in?

Agent Smith: SWAT agents engage in continuous and rigorous training to maintain their skills. This includes regular physical fitness routines, live-fire exercises, and scenario-based drills. We also train in specialized areas such as tactical driving, explosive breaching, and advanced medical response. Continuous training ensures that we are always prepared to handle high-risk operations effectively and safely.

Interviewer: What advice would you give to someone aspiring to join the FBI SWAT team?

Agent Smith: My advice would be to first focus on excelling as an FBI Special Agent. Gain extensive field experience, stay in top physical condition, and continuously develop your tactical and decision-making skills. Dedication, perseverance, and a strong commitment to serving and protecting others are essential. It's a challenging path, but it's incredibly rewarding for those who are committed and passionate.

Interviewer: Thank you for sharing these insights, Agent Smith. Your work is truly commendable.

Agent Smith: Thank you. It's an honor to serve and protect, and I appreciate the opportunity to share a bit about the process.

Chapter 4: Undercover Operation in the FBI

Undercover operations represent one of the most intriguing and perilous aspects of the FBI's investigative arsenal. These covert activities require agents to assume false identities, immerse themselves in criminal environments, and gather critical intelligence without arousing suspicion. The intricacies and dangers associated with undercover work necessitate meticulous preparation, psychological resilience, and exceptional skill.

The history of undercover operations in the FBI dates back to the early 20th century, evolving significantly over the decades. Initially, these operations were rudimentary, relying heavily on the natural guile and courage of individual agents. However, as criminal enterprises became more sophisticated, so too did the FBI's undercover tactics. The establishment of specialized training programs and the development of advanced technological tools have vastly enhanced the effectiveness of these operations.

Before embarking on an undercover mission, agents undergo extensive preparation and training. This includes studying the target organization, mastering the nuances of their assumed identities, and learning specific skills pertinent to the operation. Psychological training is also crucial, as agents must be able to maintain their cover under extreme stress and navigate the moral ambiguities inherent in such assignments. The FBI Academy offers rigorous programs that simulate real-world scenarios, ensuring agents are well-equipped to handle the complexities of undercover work.

Undercover agents employ a variety of tactics and techniques to infiltrate criminal organizations. These include establishing fake businesses, creating elaborate backstories, and using covert communication methods to relay information to their handlers. The success of an undercover operation often hinges on the agent's ability to convincingly inte-

The psychological toll of undercover work cannot be overstated. Agents must constantly balance the dual identities they inhabit, often over extended periods. The stress of living a lie, coupled with the potential for exposure and retaliation, can lead to significant emotional strain. The FBI provides robust support systems, including counseling and debriefing sessions, to help agents cope with these challenges and maintain their mental well-being.

Several high-profile cases highlight the impact and importance of undercover operations in the FBI's mission. For instance, the ABSCAM operation in the late 1970s and early 1980s, where agents posed as representatives of a fictitious Arab sheikh, led to the conviction of several politicians on corruption charges. More recently, operations targeting organized crime syndicates, drug trafficking networks, and terrorist cells have underscored the critical role of undercover work in national security and law enforcement.

Undercover operations raise significant ethical questions. The deceptive nature of these activities, while necessary, must be balanced against the potential for entrapment and the violation of individuals' rights. The FBI adheres to strict guidelines and oversight mechanisms to ensure that undercover operations are conducted legally and ethically, with a focus on minimizing collateral damage and upholding justice.

Undercover operations are a vital component of the FBI's efforts to combat crime and protect national security. The courage and ingenuity of undercover agents, combined with rigorous training and ethical oversight, enable the FBI to infiltrate and dismantle some of the most dangerous criminal organizations in the world.

Chapter 5: NIBRS andOperational Technology Division (NIBRS)

The National Incident-Based Reporting System (NIBRS) is a transformative initiative by the FBI designed to enhance the quality and comprehensiveness of crime data in the United States. Implemented to improve the overall quality of crime data collected by law enforcement, NIBRS captures details on each individual crime incident and the separate offenses within the same incident. This includes information on victims, known offenders, relationships between victims and offenders, arrestees, and property involved in crimes.

Unlike the traditional Summary Reporting System (SRS) of the Uniform Crime Reporting (UCR) Program, which provides an aggregate monthly tally of crimes, NIBRS offers a deeper and more detailed view. It provides context and circumstances for crimes, such as location, time of day, and whether the incident was cleared. This level of detail allows for a more nuanced understanding of crime patterns and trends.

Professional law enforcement organizations have recommended NIBRS for its ability to provide more useful statistics that promote constructive discussion, measured planning, and informed policing. Recognizing this, the FBI has made the nationwide implementation of NIBRS a top priority. To increase participation, the UCR Program has partnered with the Bureau of Justice Statistics on the National Crime Statistics Exchange and worked with advocacy groups to emphasize the importance of NIBRS data. As of January 1, 2021, the UCR Program has transitioned to a NIBRS-only data collection system.

To support agencies in transitioning to NIBRS, the FBI has made resources available to help address the associated costs. Additionally, there is an emphasis on educating agencies and the public that the apparent increase in crime levels under NIBRS does not indicate a rise in crime but rather a new baseline that more accurately captures reported crime in a community.

NIBRS collects data on 52 distinct offenses categorized into 24 major groups, covering a wide array of criminal activities. This detailed data collection helps law enforcement agencies, researchers, and policymapolicymakers gain a comprehensive understanding of crime dynamics, facilitating more effective strategies and policies.

The meticulous validation processes ensure the reliability and completeness of the data. Incident reports undergo both automated checks and manual reviews to meet stringent accuracy standards, underpinning informed decision-making and enhancing the credibility of crime statistics.

NIBRS's ability to capture detailed context and circumstances around each crime incident allows for the generation of in-depth reports. These reports provide valuable insights into crime patterns and trends, aiding law enforcement agencies in developing targeted strategies and offering indispensable information for researchers and policymakers.

Advanced technological systems are used for efficient data processing, storage, and analysis. The FBI continuously updates its technological infrastructure, incorporating the latest advancements to enhance the system's capabilities and ensure the timely and accurate generation of reports.

The FBI provides extensive training and support to law enforcement agencies, including workshops, webinars, and detailed instructional materials. This ensures agencies can effectively collect, validate, and submit NIBRS data, facilitating a smooth transition and ongoing compliance with NIBRS standards.

NIBRS fosters collaboration among local, state, and federal law enforcement agencies by enabling seamless data sharing. This collaborative framework enhances coordination and cooperation in addressing crime, allowing agencies to share detailed crime data, identify trends, allocate resources more efficiently, and develop coordinated responses to crime.

NIBRS represents a significant advancement in crime data reporting, enhancing public safety through detailed and reliable information. The FBI's commitment to NIBRS underscores its vital role in modernizing crime data collection and reporting, ultimately contributing to more in-cooperation in addressing crime, allowing agencies to share detailed crime data, identify trends, allocate resources more efficiently, and develop coordinated responses to crime.

NIBRS represents a significant advancement in crime data reporting, enhancing public safety through detailed and reliable information. The FBI's commitment to NIBRS underscores its vital role in modernizing crime data collection and reporting, ultimately contributing to more informed and effective crime prevention and response strategies.

(OTD)

Roles and responsibilities within the FBI's Operational Technology Division (OTD):

The Operational Technology Division (OTD) is a dynamic entity within the FBI, comprising a multidisciplinary team of professionals whose collective expertise is instrumental in advancing the agency's technological capabilities.

1. Software Engineers: These highly skilled individuals are at the forefront of software development, crafting bespoke solutions tailored to the FBI's unique operational requirements. From designing intuitive user interfaces to implementing robust backend systems, software engineers play a pivotal role in enhancing the efficiency and effectiveness of investigative processes.

2. Cybersecurity Specialists: In an era marked by escalating cyber threats, cybersecurity specialists within OTD are tasked with safeguarding the FBI's digital infrastructure against malicious actors. Through continuous monitoring, threat detection, and incident response, they fortify network defenses and mitigate cyber risks, ensuring the integrity and confidentiality of sensitive information.

3. Forensic Analysts: Forensic analysts possess specialized knowledge in digital forensics, leveraging cutting-edge tools and techniques to extract actionable intelligence from electronic devices and digital evidence. By meticulously analyzing data trails and reconstructing digital timelines, they provide invaluable support to FBI investigators in solving complex cases and prosecuting offenders.

4. Data Scientists: Data scientists harness the power of big data analytics to uncover hidden insights and patterns within vast troves of information. Through advanced statistical analysis and machine learning algorithms, they identify trends, anomalies, and correlations that inform strategic decision-making and predictive modeling, aiding in the prevention and detection of criminal activities.

5. Electronics Engineers: Electronics engineers design and develop innovative hardware solutions to support the FBI's surveillance and investigative efforts. From covert surveillance devices to specialized forensic tools, their creations enable agents to gather intelligence and gather evidence discreetly and effectively, staying one step ahead of adversaries.

6. Project Managers: Project managers oversee the planning, execution, and delivery of technology initiatives within OTD, ensuring that projects are completed on time, within budget, and according to specifications. By coordinating cross-functional teams and managing resources effectively, they facilitate collaboration and drive innovation across the division.

7. Technical Support Specialists: Technical support specialists provide frontline assistance to FBI personnel, resolving technical issues and ensuring the smooth operation of IT systems and applications. Their expertise in troubleshooting and problem-solving ensures minimal downtime and maximum productivity, enabling agents to focus on their investigative duties without interruption.

Through the collective efforts of these dedicated professionals, the Operational Technology Division (OTD) empowers the FBI with the tools, technologies, and expertise needed to combat evolving threats and uphold national security in an increasingly digital world.

Chapter 6:
Weapons of Mass Destruction (WMDs)

Weapons of Mass Destruction (WMDs) encompass nuclear, chemical, biological, and radiological materials, representing an overarching threat to both national and international security. Their catastrophic potential underscores the paramount concern they pose, necessitating an unwavering commitment from global security forces. Among these, the FBI stands as the primary federal agency in the United States tasked with confronting this multifaceted threat. With a resolute focus on safeguarding citizens and maintaining peace, the FBI orchestrates a comprehensive strategy to address the WMD menace.

At the heart of the FBI's approach is a robust intelligence-gathering mechanism. Utilizing advanced surveillance technologies and human intelligence, the FBI works tirelessly to detect early signs of WMD proliferation. This involves monitoring suspicious activities, intercepting communications, and analyzing data to identify potential threats. The agency's intelligence units collaborate closely with domestic and international partners, sharing critical information to thwart WMD-related plots before they materialize.

Collaboration with other agencies is crucial in the fight against WMDs. The FBI partners with entities such as the Department of Homeland Security, the Department of Defense, and international bodies like Interpol and the United Nations. These alliances facilitate the sharing of expertise, resources, and intelligence. Joint task forces are established to conduct coordinated operations, combining the strengths of multiple agencies to address the complexities of WMD threats.

The FBI's strategy extends beyond intelligence and collaboration to encompass proactive countermeasures. These include stringent regulations, comprehensive surveillance, and targeted interventions. The agency employs cutting-edge technologies such as radiation detection systems, bio-surveillance networks, and chemical sensors to monitor and neutralize threats. Through continuous training programs, FBI personnel remain adept at handling emerging technologies and evolving tactics used by those seeking to develop or deploy WMDs.

Forming strategic alliances is a cornerstone of the FBI's approach to WMD threats. By engaging with international allies, the FBI ensures a global network of support and intelligence sharing. Regular training exercises and simulations with allied nations enhance preparedness and foster a united front against WMD proliferation. These alliances also enable the FBI to extend its reach, intercepting threats far beyond U.S. borders.

Detecting and disrupting networks involved in WMD proliferation is a critical mission for the FBI. Specialized units focus on identifying key figures, tracking financial transactions, and uncovering clandestine operations related to WMDs. Through meticulous investigations and covert operations, these units work to dismantle networks before they can pose a significant threat. The FBI's proactive stance is pivotal in neutralizing potential dangers at their inception.

Despite extensive preventative measures, the potential for WMD incidents necessitates a robust rapid response capability. The FBI maintains specialized teams equipped to handle WMD crises, including hazardous materials experts, bomb squads, and medical response units. These teams are trained to operate in high-risk environments, employing sophisticated techniques to mitigate the impact of WMD incidents swiftly and effectively. Their readiness ensures that any breach of security can be contained and resolved with minimal casualties.

The FBI's efforts in combating WMDs extend beyond mere prevention. The agency is committed to mitigating the consequences of WMD incidents through comprehensive response plans and recovery operations. By conducting regular drills and simulations, the FBI ensures that all personnel and partnering agencies are prepared for the worst-case scenarios. This preparedness includes medical response, decontamination procedures, and public communication strategies to manage the aftermath of a WMD event.

The relentless pursuit of those seeking to develop, distribute, or deploy WMDs is a testament to the FBI's dedication to national security. Through continuous innovation, rigorous enforcement of laws, and unwavering vigilance, the FBI remains at the forefront of the fight against WMD proliferation. The agency's commitment to protecting citizens and preserving global peace is evident in every facet of its operations, reflecting a profound understanding of the grave dangers posed by WMDs.

Looking ahead, the FBI continues to adapt and evolve in response to the ever-changing landscape of WMD threats. Investment in research and development of new technologies, enhancement of international partnerships, and ongoing training programs ensure that the FBI is always prepared to meet emerging challenges. The agency's proactive stance, combined with its strategic vision, positions it as a formidable force in the ongoing effort to prevent and respond to the threat of Weapons of Mass Destruction.

In conclusion, the FBI's comprehensive approach to addressing WMD threats—through intelligence gathering, interagency collaboration, proactive countermeasures, and rapid response capabilities—demonstrates its unwavering commitment to national and international security. The relentless pursuit of those who seek to wield WMDs ensures that the FBI remains vigilant and prepared to protect citizens and uphold peace in an increasingly complex world.

Chatper 7: The Behavioral Analysis Unit of the FBI

The Behavioral Analysis Unit (BAU) is a specialized division within the FBI's National Center for the Analysis of Violent Crime (NCAVC). This unit employs behavioral analysts to assist in criminal investigations, providing critical support through their expertise in behavioral science, research, and training. The BAU's primary mission is to deliver investigative and operational support by applying behavioral-based insights to complex, time-sensitive crimes, particularly those involving violence or threats of violence.

The BAU handles a diverse array of cases across the United States, including terrorism, cybercrime, and violent offenses against both children and adults. They offer their expertise on new investigations, ongoing cases, and cold cases, working in close collaboration with federal, state, local, and tribal law enforcement agencies. The unit's tasks encompass:

1. Criminal Investigative Analysis: Evaluating the offender's motives, victim selection, sophistication level, actions, and crime sequence.
2. Interview Tactics: Utilizing behavioral science principles, psychological theories, and scientifically based approaches to design and conduct interviews.
3. Investigative Approaches: Providing behaviorally informed recommendations to enhance investigation efficiency and resource allocation.
4. Threat Evaluations: Using data-driven techniques to assess cognitive patterns and behaviors, predicting the likelihood and extent of an individual's potential for targeted violence.

The BAU originated as the Behavioral Science Unit in 1972, part of the NCAVC. It has since evolved and now comprises several distinct units under the Investigations & Operations Support Section of the FBI's Critical Incident Response Group. These units are:

- Behavioral Analysis Unit 1: Focuses on counterterrorism, arson, and bombings.
- Behavioral Analysis Unit 2: Deals with threats, cybercrime, and public corruption.
- Behavioral Analysis Unit 3: Specializes in crimes against children, providing critical support through criminal investigative analysis and working with programs like the Violent Crimes Against Children (VCAC).
- Behavioral Analysis Unit 4: Concentrates on crimes against adults and operates the Violent Criminal Apprehension Program (ViCAP).
- Behavioral Analysis Unit 5: Engages in research, strategy, and instruction, enhancing law enforcement capabilities through training and strategic advisement.

Each BAU focuses on different aspects of behavioral analysis and criminal investigation, ensuring a comprehensive approach to various types of crime.

The BAU's operations are grounded in preventing targeted violence by identifying concerning behaviors. For instance, active shooters often exhibit identifiable behaviors during their planning stages. The BAU assists law enforcement agencies through on-site consultations, conference calls, and detailed crime analyses. Their services include crime analysis, offender profiling, threat analysis, critical incident analysis, interview strategies, major case management, search warrant assistance, prosecution and trial strategies, and expert testimony.

The BAU has gained significant public attention through its depiction in popular culture. Television shows like Criminal Minds and *Mindhunter, as well as films based on Thomas Harris' Hannibal Lecter series, have dramatized the work of the BAU, bringing the intricate and crucial work of behavioral analysts into the public eye. These representations, while sometimes fictionalized, underscore the importance and impact of the BAU's work in solving and preventing violent crimes.

Despite its success, the field of criminal investigative analysis faces ongoing debates regarding its methodologies and the qualifications of its practitioners. The balance between empirical evidence and the intuition of seasoned investigators is a point of contention. Continuous research and evaluation are essential to refine profiling techniques and ensure their scientific validity and practical applicability.

In conclusion, the FBI's Behavioral Analysis Unit stands at the forefront of applying behavioral science to criminal investigations. Through their extensive expertise and collaborative efforts, they play a vital role in enhancing public safety and bringing perpetrators of violent crimes to justice.

Chapter 8: The FBI Laboratory

The FBI Laboratory is renowned for its scientific rigor and world-class expertise in solving crimes and preventing terrorism. By examining DNA, analyzing fingerprints left at crime scenes, and linking bomb fragments to terrorists, the laboratory plays a crucial role in the criminal justice system.
Law enforcement agencies can access comprehensive information about the FBI Laboratory's services through the FBI's dedicated law enforcement site, ensuring they are well-informed about the support and resources available.
The FBI boasts elite teams skilled in evidence collection, guided by subject matter experts who provide extensive training, resources, and support. These teams operate in various challenging environments:

- Underwater Operations: The FBI's forensic divers are trained to retrieve evidence from submerged environments, ensuring the integrity and preservation of crucial evidence.
- Confined Spaces: Specialized teams handle evidence collection in tight, confined areas where conventional methods are impractical.
- Remote Locations: Forensic experts are equipped to access and gather evidence from isolated and hard-to-reach areas.
- Hazardous Materials: In situations involving chemical, biological, radiological, and nuclear (CBRN) threats, technical hazards response experts ensure safe evidence collection.

Additional forensic response experts, along with FBI photographers, provide detailed crime scene surveys, comprehensive documentation, various photography techniques, and the creation of 2D and 3D models. These resources are essential for supporting FBI investigations and aiding partner law enforcement agencies in prosecution.
Evidence Response Teams (ERT) are crucial in bridging the gap between crime scenes and the FBI Laboratory. Their specialized training focuses

on meticulous scene processing to ensure every piece of evidence is collected with precision and care. These teams learn to handle diverse situations, from routine crime scenes to those involving complex and hazardous conditions.

The scope of scientific analysis at the FBI Laboratory is vast, with nearly anything connected to a crime scene providing potential clues. Some key analysis techniques include:

- Cryptanalysis: Decoding encrypted messages that may provide critical information about criminal activities.
- Document Analysis: Examining documents for authenticity, alterations, and content to uncover vital evidence.
- Trace Evidence: Analyzing small materials, such as hair, fibers, and paint, that can link suspects or victims to crime scenes.
- Latent Prints: Identifying fingerprints that are not visible to the naked eye but can be crucial in linking individuals to a crime.
- Chemistry: Conducting chemical analyses to identify substances found at crime scenes, such as drugs or explosives.

DNA analysis is a cornerstone of forensic science at the FBI Laboratory. By comparing DNA from evidence samples with reference samples from known individuals, forensic scientists can establish connections between victims, suspects, and crime scenes. This powerful tool helps to confirm or refute involvement in criminal activities.

Established in 1932, the FBI Laboratory is one of the largest and most comprehensive crime labs globally. The Laboratory Division is dedicated to employing scientific rigor in solving cases and preventing acts of crime and terrorism. It offers a wide range of services, from basic evidence analysis to advanced forensic techniques. Law enforcement partners can explore the FBI Laboratory's extensive offerings through the FBI's law enforcement site.

The FBI maintains vast collections of criminal records and other law enforcement information, including fingerprints, palm prints, and iris scans. These records are invaluable in investigations, enabling law enforcement agencies to identify and track individuals involved in criminal activities. Law enforcement partners have access to these tools, enhancing their investigative capabilities.

The FBI's Technical Hazards Response team ensures safe access to complex and dangerous crime scenes. These professionals maintain health and safety standards, allowing responders to gather evidence securely. They are equipped to handle treacherous environments, such as:

- Rocky Terrain: Navigating and collecting evidence in rugged and uneven landscapes.
- Underwater: Conducting underwater searches and evidence retrieval in various aquatic environments.

Operational technology experts at the FBI provide advanced technical capabilities to support investigations into crime and terrorism. They specialize in exploiting digital and multimedia evidence, aiding investigations involving digital footprints. The FBI's Regional Computer Forensic Laboratories (RCFLs) are full-service forensic laboratories and training centers devoted to examining digital evidence. These facilities offer comprehensive forensic services and training to law enforcement agencies, ensuring that digital evidence is thoroughly analyzed and preserved.

The FBI Laboratory, with its dedication to scientific excellence and comprehensive forensic services, stands at the forefront of criminal investigations, providing invaluable support to law enforcement agencies nationwide.

Chapter 9: FBI Artifacts

Explore the rich history of the Federal Bureau of Investigation through its remarkable artifacts. Delve into a collection that showcases pivotal moments and emblematic items from the Bureau's past.

From the harrowing events of September 11, 2001, symbolized by fragments of steel from the World Trade Center, to the relentless pursuit of justice in high-profile criminal cases like the Brinks robbery and the kidnapping of Patty Hearst, these artifacts offer a glimpse into the FBI's relentless dedication to safeguarding the nation.

Moreover, these items highlight the ingenuity and resourcefulness of FBI agents in their investigative efforts. Whether it's the covert surveillance equipment disguised as innocuous objects or the meticulous documentation of criminal activities, each artifact tells a story of innovation and determination in the face of adversity.

As you explore this collection, remember that behind each artifact lies a tale of courage, sacrifice, and unwavering commitment to the principles of justice and integrity. These artifacts serve as reminders of the FBI's enduring legacy and its ongoing mission to protect the American people from threats both domestic and abroad.

List of Artifacts:
- 9/11 Hijacker's Car
- 9/11 Responder's Hard Hat
- 9/11 World Trade Center Steel Beam
- Alarm Clocks from 2010 Times Square Bombing Attempt
- Alvin Statuette
- Baby Face Nelson Body Armor
- Barker-Karpis Gang and Russell Gibson's Notebook
- Brian P. Regan Espionage Case

- Brick from the Palace Chop House
- Brinks Robbery Cap
- Babe Ruth Baseballs
- Chagall Oil Painting
- Concealed Camera Binoculars
- Congressional Medal of Honor Fraud
- Coors Kidnapping Ransom Note
- Criminal History of Bank Robber William Sutton
- D.B. Cooper Plane Ticket

Chapter 10: National Memorial and Museum

The memorial stands as a poignant tribute, meticulously crafted to honor the memories of those who tragically lost their lives, those who endured the harrowing ordeal and survived, and those whose lives were forever altered by the events that transpired.

While recounting the narratives of the perpetrators is an inevitable aspect, the essence lies in commemoration and the profound lessons garnered. It is a meticulous process of amalgamating these accounts, extracting insights, and weaving them into a tapestry of collective wisdom, in the fervent hope of averting or mitigating future atrocities. The stark reality remains: without diligent remembrance, humanity is perilously susceptible to the cyclical recurrence of past missteps, a stark reminder of our propensity for folly and the dire consequences thereof.

We aspire to instill a fervent ethos of collaboration across generations, emphasizing the imperative of operating within the bounds of legality and institutional frameworks when endeavoring for societal change. Witnessing the tangible outcomes of such lawful engagement underscores the efficacy of constructive, lawful activism—a cornerstone of our overarching mission.

Central to our educational mandate is elucidating the pivotal role of agencies such as the FBI amidst this saga, alongside the exemplary conduct of an ordinary highway patrolman executing his duties with commendable efficacy. This singular episode compelled government entities at every tier—municipal, state, and federal—to forge unprecedented alliances, underscoring the indispensable necessity of interagency collaboration within the intricate tapestry of our Federal Government. This emergent synergy serves as a compelling testament to the potency of unity in adversity—a profound lesson we strive to impart with utmost clarity.

The despicable assault upon a bastion of governmental authority served as a rallying cry for unity—a testament to the indomitable spirit of resilience that pervades our nation's fabric. In the crucible of adversity, disparate factions coalesced, resolutely affirming the enduring resilience of our governmental institutions. Within a mere span of two days, the Federal Credit Union resumed operations, emblematic of the unwavering commitment to continuity in the face of adversity. It was a resounding declaration that, despite concerted efforts to undermine the very foundations of our governance, the resilience of our nation remains unassailable.

In retelling this saga, we reaffirm a fundamental truth: despite the concerted efforts of malevolent actors to dismantle the bedrock of our democratic ideals, the resilience of our governmental apparatus endures. It is this very government that serves as both the bulwark against transgression and the arbiter of justice, resolutely defending its citizenry whilst holding perpetrators to account.

Panoramic view of the Oklaoma City National Memorial

The Oklahoma City National Memorial, located in Oklahoma City, Oklahoma, USA, pays tribute to the victims, survivors, rescuers, and all affected by the devastating Oklahoma City bombing on April 19, 1995. Situated on the former site of the Alfred P. Murrah Federal Building, which bore the brunt of the attack, the memorial stands as a solemn reminder of the tragic events. Authorized by President Bill Clinton through the Oklahoma City National Memorial Act of 1997 and swiftly listed on the National Register of Historic Places, the memorial is overseen by the Oklahoma City National Memorial Foundation, with assistance from National Park Service personnel in guiding visitors through its poignant narrative. Formally inaugurated on April 19, 2000, the fifth anniversary of the bombing, the memorial's museum followed suit, opening its doors on February 19, 2001.

LINKS SOURCES

https://www.fbi.gov
https://fbijobs.gov

https://www.linkedin.com/company/fbi
https://www.facebook.com/FBI

National Memorial and Museum
https://youtu.be/R1TYOo_yZ8k?si=YiHLgvJ71WJHRJLB

References

AI and Law Enforcement: Applications and Ethical Considerations. Journal of AI Research, 2023.
Enhancing Public Safety with AI. National Security Journal, 2022.
Cybersecurity Framework Implementation Guide. National Institute of Standards and Technology (NIST), 2023.
Advances in Digital Forensics. Digital Forensics Magazine, 2022.
Biometric Technology in Law Enforcement. Biometric Update, 2023.
Next Generation Identification (NGI) System. FBI, 2024.
Counterterrorism Strategies in the Digital Age. Homeland Security Review, 2023.
Global Terrorism Overview. Institute for Economics and Peace, 2023.Fighting Cybercrime: The FBI's Role. Cybersecurity Ventures, 2023.
Digital Forensics Techniques. International Journal of Cybersecurity, 2022.
Combating Transnational Organized Crime. United Nations Office on Drugs and Crime (UNODC), 2023.
International Cooperation in Law Enforcement. Global Security Journal, 2022.
Community Policing and Public Trust. Policing: An International Journal, 2023.
FBI Community Outreach Programs. FBI, 2023.
Intelligence Sharing in Law Enforcement. Law Enforcement Bulletin, 2023.
Fusion Centers and Homeland Security. Department of Homeland Security, 2023.
Crime Prevention Strategies. Crime Prevention Journal, 2023.
Intervention Programs for At-Risk Youth. Social Work Today, 2023.

www.ingramcontent.com/pod-product-compliance
Lightning Source LLC
Chambersburg PA
CBHW060033180426
43196CB00045B/2638